THE BEATLES

THIS IS A CARLTON BOOK

Published in Great Britain in 2014 by
Carlton Books Limited
20 Mortimer Street
London W1T 3JW

Some of the text in this book was previously published as
The Beatles Encyclopedia and *Treasures of The Beatles* by
Carlton Books Limited.

A CIP catalogue record of this book can be obtained from the
British Library.

ISBN 978-1-78097-601-3

Printed in China

10 9 8 7 6 5 4 3 2

THE
BEATLES

Terry Burrows

CARLTON
BOOKS

CONTENTS

8 1957–60

10 1961

16 1962

18 1963

22 *PLEASE PLEASE ME*

24 JOHN LENNON

30 *WITH THE BEATLES*

32 1964

38 *A HARD DAY'S NIGHT*

40 *BEATLES FOR SALE*

44 PAUL MCCARTNEY

48 1965

50 *HELP!*

52 *RUBBER SOUL*

54 1966

58 *REVOLVER*

60 1967

62 *SGT. PEPPER'S LONELY HEARTS CLUB BAND*

66 GEORGE HARRISON

70 1968

74 *THE BEATLES (THE WHITE ALBUM)*

78 *YELLOW SUBMARINE*

80 RINGO STARR

84 1969

86 *ABBEY ROAD*

90 *LET IT BE*

92 1970

94 DISCOGRAPHY

Left: The Beatles in 1963: Paul McCartney, George Harrison, Ringo Starr and John Lennon.

Overleaf: The classic leap photograph, shot in 1963, was used on the group's *Twist & Shout* EP.

1957-1960 ENTER THE BEATLES

Faced with another dull city summer, a young Liverpool lad named John Lennon had found a way around the boredom. His skiffle group, the Quarrymen, were named after the school he loathed. They played wherever they could find an audience, although they were rarely received with enthusiasm.

Below: The Silver Beetles on stage in 1960 in Liverpool. The drummer Johnny Hutch was sitting in – they didn't have a regular drummer at the time.

THE FAB THREE

On July 6, 1957, the Quarrymen played St Peter's Parish church fete in Woolton. Ivan Vaughan came just to watch, bringing with him a friend from the Liverpool Institute. He wanted John to meet his friend – Paul McCartney. John and Paul's first meeting started out as a cool affair, until Paul revealed a winning secret – he could tune a guitar. John and Paul gradually spent more and more time together. Despite very different personalities they shared a love of music and guitars. The other Quarrymen were unconvinced, finding McCartney bossy and big-headed.

Skiffle had been a short-lived fad. Rock and roll was the real thing: rising stars like Eddie Cochran were not only brilliant performers, they also wrote their own songs. John and Paul also started to create new material, becoming extremely competitive with one another.

Around the same time, Paul befriended another pupil at the Liverpool Institute. George Harrison was nearly two years younger and, aged just 14, he began following the band. Always at their gigs, guitar in hand, John would even let him take the odd solo. George, however, had a trick up his sleeve – he had a place to rehearse at weekends. George gradually eased himself into The Quarrymen.

THE SILVER BEETLES

By the start of 1960, the Quarrymen comprised just John, Paul and George. John, now at art school, met a fellow student,

quit music immediately afterwards. Williams had placed a pair of bands in a German nightclub, and was now in need of a third. The Beatles – as the Silver Beetles now insisted on being called – seemed viable. The band members leapt at the chance. As drummer, they recruited acquaintance Pete Best, who they knew from their time in his mother's venue, the Casbah Coffee Club. Then they charged off to Hamburg.

THE GERMAN ADVENTURE

Germany was a trial by fire for The Beatles. Initially, the band worked on a cramped stage in the miniscule Indra club, and lived together in one small, noisy room above a cinema across the road. Regular four-hour sets left everyone exhausted. The band gradually attracted a small following, John's manic stage capering an early focal point. When the Indra was closed down because of noise complaints the band moved to the owner's other club, the Kaiserkeller. Here they worked alongside fellow Williams placements Rory Storm and the Hurricanes. Rory's flamboyant drummer, Richard Starkey wore gaudy rings on every finger, and was known to everyone as Ringo Starr.

Gradually friendships formed between the bands. When the Hurricanes' bass player Lou Walters wanted to cut a record as a singer, John, Paul and George went to help. Ringo was there too. It was the first time the four ever played together. Stu meanwhile had made a number of artist friends, including a talented photographer and artist, Astrid Kirchherr. The two quickly fell in love, and it was Kirchherr who suggested The Beatles needed a style. She made them clothes and invented the famous mop-top look, complete with matching hairstyle.

Things were starting to look up. Towards the end of their

Kaiserkeller gig, the band were offered a much better deal at the Top Ten club. They accepted, but the Kaiserkeller's owner was furious and took his own revenge: a 'surprise' police passport check the next day revealed that George was underage, and he was immediately deported. A few days later John and Paul were booted out too, for a minor accidental arson incident. Stu had little choice but to follow. It was a bleak moment.

Meet The Quarrymen

By the middle of 1957, John Lennon was well ensconced in the rock and roll lifestyle. Mustering all the enthusiasm they had failed to put into their school work, Lennon and his close friend Pete Shotton – Quarry Bank Grammar School's resident teenage rebels – had gathered a growing number of enthusiasts: Nigel Whalley and Ivan Vaughan, who shared duties on the tea-chest bass; Rod Davis, whose parents had just bought him a banjo; guitarist Eric Griffiths; and drummer Colin Hanton. Shotton played the washboard. Lennon played his beloved guitar.

The Quarrymen performed covers of Lonnie Donegan songs and American rock and roll hits. They got engagements at school dances and youth clubs, but were rarely received with any great enthusiasm. Although there were differing views on the direction they should take, there was no disputing that John Lennon was the boss.

Above left: Stuart Sutcliffe and Astrid Kirchherr. Stu played bass with The Beatles for two years. He left the group to study art – his principal passion.

Above: Autograph book containing the signatures of Johnny Gentle (the headline act) and the Silver Beetles. Paul's signature, 'Paul Ramon', can be seen – the pseudonym inspired the 1970s punk band The Ramones. The drummer at the time was Tommy Moore.

a brilliant artist named Stuart Sutcliffe. They quickly became close friends, John persuading Stu to buy a bass guitar and join the band. Local promoter Allan Williams gave them some gigs at his tiny Jacaranda club, and found them a drummer, 36-year-old professional Tommy Moore. It was Moore who recommended a proper name – something like Buddy Holly's Crickets. Stu jokingly suggested the Beetles, which John twisted to Beatles. Everyone at the Jacaranda hated that, and they became the Silver Beetles.

When Billy Fury needed a backing group, the Silver Beetles tried out. They didn't get the job, but Larry Parnes, the impresario behind Fury, was impressed enough to offer them a tour of Scotland with another singer, Johnny Gentle. The tour wasn't long, but Moore was injured on only the second night. He managed to limp through, but

ENTER BRIAN STAGE LEFT

Unceremoniously ejected from Hamburg, The Beatles were surprised to find a burgeoning beat scene awaiting them back home. Furthermore, their reputation had spread back to Liverpool via the other Mersey bands who had done similar stints in Hamburg. The Beatles had left Liverpool as a bunch of enthusiastic also-rans, but returned as one of the city's hottest acts.

Ray McFall, the owner of the Cavern club, had noticed the popularity of the new beat groups. A Beatles gig at Mona Best's Casbah club in December 1960 persuaded him to give them a shot. The Beatles became regulars there in February. They were given 25 shillings (£1.25) a day to play two 45-minute stints – an easy task compared to Hamburg. They quickly became a big attraction. And the girls soon started screaming.

Things were going well, but Stu Sutcliffe began to feel more and more of an outsider. He missed Astrid, and also realised that he was the weak link in a good band. Paul didn't disagree. He was tiring of Stu's limitations, and was ready to take over the bass. In retrospect, Paul regrets some of his behaviour towards Stu: "Perhaps I could have dealt with him more sensitively, but then who's sensitive at that age? Certainly not me!"

In March 1961, singer Tony Sheridan asked the band to go back out to Hamburg for a few months. This time, playing at the Top Ten club, they were earning twice as much as before – £40 each per week, considerably more than back home. It was hard work, though. The sets started at 7pm, and they alternated with Sheridan until 3am.

EXIT STU

Stu was ecstatic to be back with Astrid, but increasingly unenthusiastic about The Beatles. She encouraged him to

enrol at the Hamburg State Art College to study under Eduardo Paolozzi, one of Stu's idols. Paolozzi was highly impressed by his work, and even arranged him a state bursary. Stu gradually began to step back from the band. He never formally left – Paul gradually played the bass more and more, until one day he played bass all the time.

Germany was yet to sign up wholeheartedly to the idea of rock 'n' roll. But interest was growing. Bert Kaempfert, a well-known orchestral band leader turned producer, found Sheridan and The Beatles playing at the Top Ten and asked them to make a rather unusual record. 'My Bonnie Lies Over The Ocean', an age-old Scottish folk song, was the A-side; the flip side was 'When the Saints Go Marching In'. Both were recorded in a beat-group style with Tony Sheridan singing. 'My Bonnie' by 'The Beat Brothers' hit the top ten in Germany and turned Sheridan into a minor star; The Beatles received session payments of £25 each. However it was soon to prove far more valuable.

"RIGHT THEN BRIAN, MANAGE US"

Back in Liverpool in July, the beat revolution was everywhere. There was even a Liverpool music paper – *Mersey Beat*, started by art student Bill Harry. John, an old pal of his, did a humorous article, "A Short Diversion on the Dubious Origins of The Beatles", for the first edition. One of the paper's main distributors was North East Musical Stores – NEMS, as it was

Above: Manager Brian Epstein, the first manager of The Beatles.

known. Under the management of the owner's son, Brian Epstein, its Charlotte Street branch had become one of the best record shops in the Liverpool area. Brian became curious when an order came in for a copy of 'My Bonnie' by The Beatles. His PA, Alistair Taylor, told him that they were a local band that played regularly at the Cavern Club. [There is some suggestion that Taylor, in fact, planted the order himself to drum up some interest in the band.]

On November 9 Brian Epstein decided to check The Beatles out for himself, and Bill Harry arranged for him to meet the band after their show. Brian was taken aback by what he saw: "This was quite a new world really for me. I was amazed by this dank atmosphere … they [The Beatles] were somewhat ill-clad and the presentation left a little to be desired. Amongst this, however, something tremendous came over. I was really just struck by their music, the beat and their sense of humour on stage. Even afterwards, when I met them, I was struck again by their personal charm. It was there it all started."

Brian made several more visits to the Cavern Club and finally, on December 10, offered to manage The Beatles. The band agreed.

The Beatles were now at the top of the Mersey Beat pile, but were largely unknown outside of the immediate area. Brian knew they had to get the attention of the big London record companies. He was confident of getting an audition, though – as the manager of one of the biggest record stockists in the north, no label would want to risk unnecessarily upsetting such a valuable client. As far as Brian Epstein was concerned, all he had to do was get the labels to hear the band – their music would do the talking. 1962 was going to be interesting.

Right: *Mersey Beat* newspaper, a local Liverpool publication.

Above: Stuart Sutcliffe in moody rocker pose. Photograph by Astrid Kirchherr.

Overleaf: Pete Best, George Harrison, John Lennon, Paul McCartney and Stuart Sutcliffe pictured at a Hamburg funfair. Photograph by Astrid Kirchherr.

The Cavern Club

The Cavern Club, 10 Mathew Street, Liverpool, opened on January 16, 1957. Its founder was Alan Sytner, a lifelong jazz enthusiast, who chose the former air-raid shelter as a venue after visiting the famous cellar jazz club Le Caveau de la Huchette in Paris. Financial problems, partly due to trying to fix the underground venue's shortcomings, led him to sell up in 1959. Ray McFall, who worked for Sytner's accountant, took it over and turned it towards rock 'n' roll. The Beatles made their first group appearance there on February 21, 1961 – a lunchtime concert. By the time of their last appearance two years later, on August 3, 1963, they had become stars.

The club closed in 1973, and was demolished. It was recreated in 1984 by former Liverpool footballer Tommy Smith, using as much of the original space and brickwork as possible. It closed for 18 months in 1989, and re-opened in 1991 run by two mates, teacher Bill Heckle and cabbie Dave Jones. They still run the club today, as a live music venue most nights of the week. Touring bands – including Oasis and The Arctic Monkeys – sometimes use it as a 'secret' warm-up venue, and Paul McCartney played his last gig of the last millennium there on December 14, 1999.

Would there have been a Beatles – or a Mersey Beat movement – without the Cavern?

'Swinging Lunch Time Rock Sessions'
AT THE
LIVERPOOL JAZZ SOCIETY,
13, TEMPLE STREET (off Dale Street and Victoria Street),
EVERY LUNCH TIME, 12-00 to 2-30
RESIDENT BANDS:

Gerry and the Pacemakers,
Rory Storm and the Wild Ones,
The Big Three.

Next Wednesday Afternoon, March 15th
12-00 to 5-00 Special
STARRING—

The Beatles,
Gerry and the Pacemakers
Rory Storm and the Wild Ones.

Admission—Members 1/-, Visitors 1/6

" Rocking at the L. J. S. "

The Victor Printing Co 230, West Derby Road, Liverpool, 6

THE BEATLES

Above: Set list on autographed promo card, 1963.

Left: Liverpool Jazz Society flyer, 1961

14

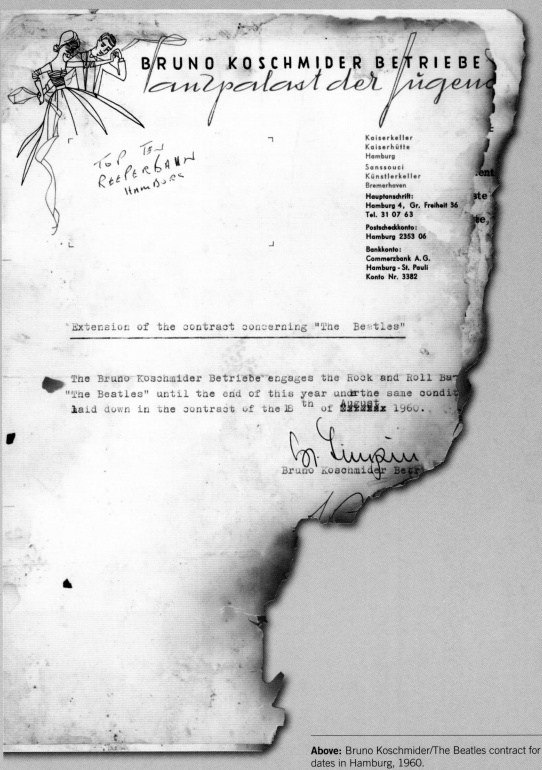

ADDITIONAL CLAUSES

1) Should either The Beatles break the contract they will compensate Mr. Koschmider in full

2) Should Mr. Koschmider break the contract he will be held liable to pay the full fee of engagement for tour.

3) Mr. Koschmider to set working permits for The Beatles.

PLAYING TIMES

Tuesday to Friday playing times 4 1/2 hours
pm to 9-30 pm, break 1/2 hour. 10-00 pm to 11-00 pm break 1/2 hour
1-30 to 12-30 am break 1/2 hour. 1 00 am to 2 am.

Saturday playing times 6 hours
00 pm to 8-30 pm break 1/2 hour. 9-00 pm to 10-00 pm break 1/2 hour
-30 pm to 11-30 pm break 1/2 hour. 12-00 to 1-00 am break 1/2 hour
00 am to 3-00 am.

Sunday playing times 6 houres
pm to 6-00 pm break 1/2 hour. 6-30 to 7-30 pm 1/2 hour break.
to 9-00 pm break 1/2 hour. 9-30 to 10-30 pm break 1/2 hour.
to 12.00 pm break 1/2 hour. 12-30 to 1-30 am

Must agree to aside to the conditions laid out in contract.

BRUNO KOSCHMIDER BETRIEBE

Tanzpalast der Jugend

TOP TEN
REEPERBAHN
HAMBURG

Kaiserkeller
Kaiserhütte
Hamburg

Sanssouci
Künstlerkeller
Bremerhaven

Hauptanschrift:
Hamburg 4, Gr. Freiheit 36
Tel. 31 07 63

Postscheckkonto:
Hamburg 2353 06

Bankkonto:
Commerzbank A. G.
Hamburg - St. Pauli
Konto Nr. 3382

Extension of the contract concerning "The Beatles"

The Bruno Koschmider Betriebe engages the Rock and Roll Ba
"The Beatles" until the end of this year under the same condit
laid down in the contract of the 18 th of August 1960.

Bruno Koschmider Betr

"PETE, THE BOYS WANT YOU OUT OF THE GROUP. THEY DON'T THINK YOU'RE A GOOD ENOUGH DRUMMER."

Brian Epstein's sacking of Pete Best came as quite as shock to the drummer, now famously dubbed "the unluckiest man in pop history".

Above: Bruno Koschmider/The Beatles contract for dates in Hamburg, 1960.

1962 UPS AND DOWNS

The first label Epstein tried was Decca – one of the most powerful of Britain's record companies. The audition took place at 165 Broadhurst Gardens, in West Hampstead, London on January 1, 1962. Recording processes at the time were crude by today's standards. The Beatles simply plugged in their instruments and Decca's A&R ("artist and repertoire") man Mike Smith asked them to play. In the space of a few hours, The Beatles had laid down 15 tracks. Listening to them today, the band's humour and versatility still manages to shine through.

The Beatles were not happy with their performance, but Mike Smith thought it would be enough to a secure a deal. Unfortunately, Decca had just auditioned another group – Brian Poole and the Tremeloes. From Dagenham in Essex, the Tremeloes won because they were near London, where they would be easier to control. The decision has since become legendary: in one of pop music's most celebrated errors of judgement, Smith's boss Dick Rowe informed Brian Epstein that he didn't want the band because "they sounded too much like the Shadows", but even that was irrelevant since "groups with guitars are on the way out".

Brian imposed a new, professional regime, and dressed the band in their famous grey suits. In March, he booked them to open a new venue in Hamburg, the Star Club. They were looking forward to seeing old mates, not least Stuart Sutcliffe and Astrid. John and Stu had remained close friends, corresponding frequently. But The Beatles arrived in Hamburg to terrible news: Stu was dead. He had recently suffered a spate of increasingly serious headaches, ending in a haemorrhage. The band was devastated – Pete and George cried continually. John refused to crack, but everybody knew he was by far the worst affected.

Meanwhile, Brian was busy in London trying to get them a deal. He had now taken their Decca demo to every reasonably sized label he could find. Thinking a playable disc to demo might help, Brian went to the HMV store in London's Oxford Street, where it was possible to have individual records cut from a master tape. Brian's arrival started a sequence of good fortune. The engineer who processed the record liked the band, suggesting that he take it to EMI's publishing wing. Later that same day, Sid Coleman, EMI's head of publishing, heard the disc and offered them a deal. It was a breakthrough, but Brian explained that he *really* wanted a recording contract for the band. Coleman arranged a meeting for the following week for Brian with George Martin, head of A&R for Parlophone, one of EMI's subsidiary labels.

Martin was largely unenthusiastic about beat groups, but on hearing their demo disc was just about sufficiently interested to offer an audition. The session took place on June 6, 1962 at EMI's Abbey Road studios, a large detached house in the middle of St John's Wood, an up-market area of north London. The only surviving original song from the session was a new composition, 'Love Me Do'.

Above: During 1962, The Beatles played frequently at the Star Club in Hamburg, Germany.

Opposite above: The Beatles perform one of their last gigs with drummer Pete Best.

Opposite below: Portrait of music producer George Martin.

Ringo's Chilly Welcome

By the time of The Beatles' first professional recording session, Pete Best was gone. George Martin, however, had not been informed and so booked-in Andy White, his regular session drummer. Turning up with the band, Ringo was not allowed to play. The following week, Martin gave him his chance to play, and was pleasantly surprised. Whilst not as good as a seasoned session man like White, Ringo was a clear improvement on Pete Best. During the sessions they would each record alternate takes of 'Love Me Do', the song chosen as their debut single. When Andy White's version was released three weeks later, on October 4, Ringo was devastated. His version *did* make it to the album, though.

PROBLEMS WITH THE DRUMMER

Martin contemplated The Beatles for a month or so before offering them a one-year contract. He was worried about Pete Best's playing though, insisting he wasn't up to scratch. Paul and George were prepared to sack him just to get the matter out of the way. John was too absorbed with long-term girlfriend Cynthia's shock pregnancy to care either way. On Thursday, August 16, Best was called to Brian Epstein's office and given the news: "Pete, the boys want you out of the group. They don't think you're a good enough drummer." Distraught at being dropped by his mates, Best would continue to develop a musical career, but is mostly remembered as perhaps the unluckiest man in pop history. Meanwhile, the next day John and Cynthia were married.

At this time Ringo Starr was reluctantly playing the summer season at Skegness Butlins holiday camp with Rory Storm. John offered him the job of replacing Pete, and a few days later he played his first gig as a Beatle. Not everyone was happy, though: Pete had always been a big favourite with the girls. But that would soon change.

"GENTLEMEN, YOU HAVE JUST MADE YOUR FIRST NUMBER ONE"

The sessions for the first Beatles single took place on September 6 and 11. Martin had decided on original compositions. He selected two tracks: 'P.S. I Love You' and 'Love Me Do', with the latter appearing as the A-side.

Outside Liverpool, The Beatles were still largely unknown and there was little national interest in the record. Brian knew the critical importance of good sales, and bought up 10,000 copies from Parlophone through NEMS. Whilst the vast majority of those singles would remain in the NEMS

storeroom it kick-started The Beatles' chart career, 'Love Me Do' entering the *New Musical Express* chart at number 27. It was The Beatles' first national showing. The single eventually peaked at number 17, and won them a five-year deal with George Martin and Parlophone.

When it came to recording the second single at the end of November, the band flatly refused Epstein and Martin's recommended material in favour of one of their own new compositions. A gutsy number, 'Please Please Me', showed off the band's vocal harmonies to the full. George Martin knew instinctively that it was going to be a hit on a massive scale. At the end of the session he pressed the studio intercom button to speak to the band: "Gentlemen," he announced, "you have just made your first number one."

The year ended inauspiciously. Having been voted the *NME*'s fifth best British vocal group of 1962, The Beatles were contractually tied to spending Christmas and New Year stuck in the Hamburg red light district, playing the Star Club. It was the last place in the world they now wanted to be.

1963 THE YEAR WHEN EVERYTHING CHANGED

The Beatles flew back into Britain at the start of 1963. January 11 was the big day – 'Please, Please Me' was to hit the UK's record shops. Brian Epstein and Northern Songs publisher Dick James put a combined effort into publicising the new release. James was able to get The Beatles a slot on a popular Saturday night music show, *Thank Your Lucky Stars*. Broadcast on Saturday, January 19, although they were effectively bottom of the bill, The Beatles were a sensation.

Opposite: The Queen Mother talking to The Beatles after the Royal Variety Show.

The Beatles stood out a mile with their "mop-top" fringes and neat matching buttoned-up suits. But above all, The Beatles refused to appear mean and moody like so many other rock and rollers. They bounced around the television screen with beaming grins looking as if they were four lads having a fantastic time. And the sound was different, too: 'Please Please Me' was the first time the public was to experience one of the great hallmarks of the early Beatles sound: the band's dramatic use of falsetto singing. And it was clear from their TV performance that shifting the dynamic in this way had an impact on their teenage audience – it seemed to make them scream more loudly!

HITTING THE TOP SPOT

On February 10, The Beatles travelled down to London to record their debut album. They started work at Studio 2, Abbey Road at ten in the morning and carried on until eleven at night, stopping only briefly for lunch and dinner. In the space of barely 13 hours, they recorded a staggering 79 takes of 14 songs. Nowadays it would be hard to imagine a major

recording artist producing an LP within a single month let alone a single day! There was no let-up, though: the next day they went straight back to their live work – a schedule that now saw them performing in different venues throughout the country pretty much every day of the week.

Finally, on March 2, George Martin's prediction was fulfilled as 'Please Please Me' went to the top of the UK singles chart, staying there for a fortnight. Parlophone released The Beatles' debut album on March 22. To cash in on the success of the single, the album was also titled *Please Please Me*. It was an immediate success, entering the LP charts at number nine.

RIDING THE WHIRLWIND

The rest of the year was a whirlwind for the band. Mersey Beat had suddenly become big news and major London labels rushed north to see if there were other Beatles-like bands awaiting discovery. Brian Epstein took full advantage of this phenomenon and his roster of acts at NEMS soon read like a *Who's Who* of British pop in 1963.

The Mersey Beat

Brian Epstein's NEMS Enterprises typically signed up the best bands that Liverpool could produce. More than anyone else, he was responsible for commercialising the Mersey revolution. He set up an office in London, and used the success of The Beatles to find recording contracts for his other new acts. More often than not, his bands found fame performing Lennon and McCartney compositions.

Liverpool's other big success story of the time was Gerry and the Pacemakers who were generally considered to be Liverpool's 'second' band, even though they had managed to score a number one single a few weeks before The Beatles. They also achieved another feat that The Beatles failed to match: that of having their first three singles top the charts. This run began with 'How Do You Do It?', a Mitch Murray song The Beatles had already turned down! This achievement wouldn't be duplicated until the 1980s, when another Liverpool band, Frankie Goes To Hollywood, similarly topped the charts with their first three singles.

Other Mersey bands to experience success were Billy J Kramer and the Dakotas and the Fourmost — both of whom enjoyed a number of Lennon and McCartney hits. The Searchers also enjoyed a lengthy chart career, often playing unknown American hits: 'Sugar and Spice', 'Sweets for my Sweet' and 'Needles and Pins' all managed high chart placings.

Things were now moving at a pace. April saw the launch of The Beatles' third single, 'From Me To You'. After performing the song at a sell-out concert in front of 10,000 people at the *NME* Poll-Winner's Show in Wembley it also went straight to the number one spot.

Fearing that his charges were running out of steam, Brian prescribed two weeks holiday for the band. Paul, George and Ringo went to Tenerife with the girls, while John accompanied Brian to Spain. When the boys returned, they discovered that the album had also hit the number one spot.

Summer 1963 passed by in a haze of interviews and live performances. In June, John and Paul had managed to grab a few hours in a Newcastle hotel room to come up with a new song. Before the end of November, the band's fourth single, 'She Loves You', had sold over a million copies.

The Beatles achieved a new level of credibility when Don Haworth's ground-breaking documentary *Merseybeat* was broadcast at the end of October. It was filmed in Liverpool during August, and took a sociological rather than musical perspective. The Beatles and other local bands were filmed playing, chatting, preparing behind the scenes, all interlocking with enough reality to give the viewer a sense of Liverpool life at the time. It was the first time anyone had taken young people's music seriously, and it went a long way towards legitimising what was happening in pop and rock.

On November 4, The Beatles performed at the Royal Command Performance in front of the Queen and Princess Margaret, along with a selection of London's great and good. Their cheeky humour and charm won the guests over, and the Queen visibly enjoyed the show. She joked with them about their next gig, in Slough, being near her home. *The Daily Mirror's* front-page report could only manage a one-word headline – "Beatlemania".

And Beatlemania it was. The album *Please Please Me* was only toppled from the number one spot by the follow-up, *With The Beatles*. When the next single, 'I Want To Hold Your Hand', was released, over a million copies were ordered in advance. Britain belonged to The Beatles.

But America was still to come …

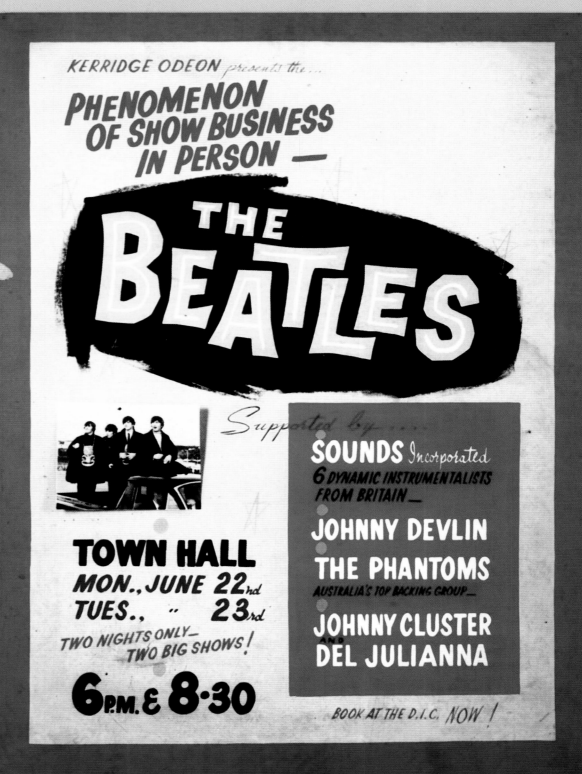

Above: Poster advertising the March 21 bill at the ABC, Croydon: The Beatles were effectively bottom of the bill.

Right: Poster for concert at the Kerridge Odeon, Wellington, New Zealand, 1964.

ON
THE
STAGE

GAUMONT - IPSWICH

Manager: P. LOWE

Telephone 53641

ONE
DAY
ONLY

WEDNESDAY, 22nd MAY at 6.35 and 8.45

Peter Walsh in association with Kennedy Street Enterprises Ltd.
and Tito Burns, presents

'PLEASE PLEASE ME'
'FROM ME TO YOU'

THE BEATLES

GERRY and the PACEMAKERS

ERKEY GRANT **IAN CRAWFORD** 'A Very Good Year for Girls' **DAVID MACBETH**

TONY MARSH **TERRY YOUNG SIX** THE LOVELY FILM AND RECORDING STAR **LOUISE CORDET** The 'I'm just a baby' Girl

From the UNITED STATES 'Only the Lonely' 'Dream Baby' 'Running Scared' 'In Dreams'

ROY ORBISON

SEATS **10/6** **9/6** **8/6** **7/6** **6/6** **5/6**

Above: The Beatles/Roy Orbison tour poster, 1963.

21

PLEASE PLEASE ME

Label: Parlophone PCS 3042
Producer: George Martin
Release: March 22, 1963

Left: John, Paul, George and Ringo parody the hysteria that now surrounds their every move.

SIDE ONE

I SAW HER STANDING THERE
(Lennon/McCartney)

This Chuck Berry-influenced song had been a part of The Beatles' live set for some time. It was written in 1961 by Paul McCartney – back then he had called it 'Seventeen'. John Lennon later came up with some additional lyrics. Paul apparently wrote the song about a girl named Iris Caldwell, whom he had dated back in Liverpool. Iris was the seventeen-year-old sister of Rory Storm. Paul sings the lead part, but John provides backing vocals in the chorus.

MISERY
(Lennon/McCartney)

John wrote this song backstage at a gig in Stoke-on-Trent. He originally intended it to be for Helen Shapiro, but she never recorded it. Instead, it was given to Kenny Lynch, a black British singer – unusual at that time – who also appeared with The Beatles as a part of the Helen Shapiro tour package. Lynch's version of 'Misery' is noteworthy as the first cover of a Lennon and McCartney song. John and Paul share the lead vocals.

ANNA (GO TO HIM)
(Alexander)

American R&B singer Arthur Alexander had recorded this song himself in 1962, but without any chart success. John, in particular, liked the song and sang lead himself.

CHAINS

(Goffin/King)

Husband and wife songwriting team Gerry Goffin and Carole King were amongst the most successful songwriters in the world in the early sixties. Carole King herself enjoyed a highly successful musical career, which peaked with her album *Tapestry*, one of the biggest sellers of the 1970s. 'Chains' had been a Top 5 hit in America for the Cookies. The Beatles' version features George on lead vocals for the first time.

BOYS

(Dixon/Farrell)

Although he would eventually enjoy a good few hits in his own right, Ringo Starr will never be remembered as one of pop's greatest singers. Here he drones his way through another song which shows The Beatles' love of American R&B, Luther Dixon and Wes Farrell's 'Boys' (originally a Shirelles B-side). This song was popular with many of the Liverpool bands; Ringo had originally sung it with Rory Storm and the Hurricanes.

ASK ME WHY

(Lennon/McCartney)

John sings this rather tame little ditty which first appeared on the flip side of 'Please Please Me'.

PLEASE PLEASE ME

(Lennon/McCartney)

The single that put The Beatles at the top of the charts. Everything about it works – the harmonica-led introduction, unusual vocal harmonies, galloping guitar chords that link the verse sections, and the falsetto chorus. John wrote 'Please Please Me' at his Aunt Mimi's house after hearing Roy Orbison sing 'Only The Lonely'.

SIDE TWO

LOVE ME DO

(Lennon/McCartney)

The band's first hit. Paul wrote the song one day when skipping school, and John contributed the middle eight. The version that appears on the album is not the same

as the single, which features George Martin's uncredited session drummer, Andy White. Ringo plays on this cut.

P.S. I LOVE YOU

(Lennon/McCartney)

The flip side of 'Love Me Do'. Paul is mainly responsible for this song, backed by George and John. Again, Andy White plays drums on this version.

BABY IT'S YOU

(David/Williams/Bacharach)

John sings lead on another song originally recorded by the Shirelles – this one had been a big US hit in 1961. It was one of Burt Bacharach's early successes. The Bacharach/David songwriting partnership went on to become one of the most important in modern music.

DO YOU WANT TO KNOW A SECRET?

(Lennon/McCartney)

John wrote this song for George to sing. He claimed the idea came from watching a Walt Disney film, either *Cinderella* or *Fantasia* – he couldn't remember which. In fact, it's more likely to have been *Snow White*, in which the heroine sings 'I'm Wishing' – the two songs have very similar first lines. 'Do You Want To Know a Secret?' was recorded as a single by another of Brian Epstein's artists, Billy J. Kramer. It went to the top of the British charts in May 1963.

A TASTE OF HONEY

(Scott/Marlowe)

One of Paul McCartney's favourite show tunes, 'A Taste of Honey' was written by Ric Marlow and Bobby Scott for the musical of the same name. Martin Denny had scored a minor hit with an unusual instrumental version of the song in 1962.

THERE'S A PLACE

(Lennon/McCartney)

Written by John, 'There's a Place' is an early example of the introversion and desire to escape that would crop up time

Above: Screaming fans await The Beatles at a concert in Manchester.

after time in his lyrics. Although not easy to detect, the song was also evidently an attempt to create a Motown type of sound. At the beginning of 1963, American soul music was beginning to take off in Europe and Motown artists such as Smokey Robinson and Marvin Gaye were amongst The Beatles' favourites.

TWIST AND SHOUT

(Medley/Russell)

Another of the most significant American black groups of the time was the Isley Brothers. 'Twist and Shout' had been the band's live show-stopper since they first heard the song. John gives a ferocious vocal performance, all the more impressive considering that this was recorded at the end of a 13-hour session, when his voice had almost gone. Ironically, the song was later taken near the top of the charts by Brian Poole and the Tremoloes – the very band who Decca had signed in preference to The Beatles.

JOHN LENNON

The city of Liverpool was the principal port in the north-west of England, and one of Europe's traditional seafaring gateways to America. That meant it wasn't the safest place to be living in the early days of the Second World War. October 9, 1940 saw a particularly fierce spate of night raids, but this was the last thing on the mind of the young Julia Lennon as she lay in Liverpool's Oxford Street Maternity Home. With bombs falling around the hospital, Julia gave birth to a boy. She decided to name him John. His second name, in honour of Britain's wartime prime minister, was Winston.

Julia was one of five daughters. Her father worked for the Glasgow and Liverpool Salvage Company – the numerous shipwrecks along the Mersey had kept him and his colleagues busy ever since the air raids had first begun. Julia was the wild one of the family. Two years earlier, she'd married long-time sweetheart Alf 'Freddy' Lennon, at least partly to defy the wishes of her father. It was not to be the closest of relationships: Freddy worked on the great passenger liners that travelled between Liverpool and New York and they were apart more often than not.

Freddy was berthed in New York when war broke out. Wanting to avoid participation at all costs he jumped ship. He was eventually interned at Ellis Island, and ended up serving a sentence for desertion at a British military prison in North Africa. Julia herself would later admit that her decision to marry Freddy was one of the least serious of her life. While Freddy returned to Liverpool for a few brief visits in 1940 – long enough to "put her in the family way" as she put it – he largely disappeared from her life from that moment onwards. Freddy did reappear briefly in 1945 and tried to persuade John and Julia to move to New Zealand with him.

The war brought hardship to everyone, but it was an especially difficult time for a young mother. Julia was not only unhappy but unsettled. She longed for the carefree times that had been possible before the war, and before she became tied down with a baby. While Julia was not exactly a 'poor' mother, much of the burden of child care fell on other members of her family. During this time it gradually became apparent that her sister Mimi was forming an especially close relationship with John. Far from causing any jealousy, Julia was relieved. As the war came to an end, life in Liverpool began to resume normality. Julia was young and attractive and there was soon a new man in her life. Working at a café in Penny Lane, she met Bobby Dykins and fell in love.

Opposite top: A rare photo of John with Julia (c.1950).

Opposite below: John Lennon (c. 1948) as a young boy in school uniform.

Julia

Julia Stanley was born on March 12, 1914, the daughter of George and Annie Stanley. She was the fourth of five children, all girls, and had a reputation for being impulsive, flighty and funny. She was also musically talented, as was her mostly absent husband, Alf 'Freddy' Lennon. Their only child together, John, was her first, but she went on to have three daughters – the first of whom she put up for adoption, under pressure.

Although John spent most of his childhood living with his aunts, especially Mimi, Julia remained close to him, keeping in very regular contact. She strongly encouraged his musical and free-spirited tendencies, and, despite Mimi's significant disapproval, bought him his first guitar. During his teenage years, John would often stay at the house Julia shared with Bobby Dykins and their two daughters, Julia and Jacqui.

Tragically, Julia was killed on July 15, 1958 by a drunk learner-driver, an off-duty policeman named Eric Clague. Drinking and driving was not illegal at that time, and Clague's testimony stated that she simply walked out of the hedge-lined central reservation straight in front of him. He was acquitted of all charges.

Julia was buried in Liverpool's Allerton Cemetary.

"BEING A TEENAGER AND MY MOTHER BEING KILLED, JUST WHEN I WAS RE-ESTABLISHING A RELATIONSHIP WITH HER ... IT WAS VERY TRAUMATIC FOR ME."

John, on the death of his mother, Julia.

AUNT MIMI

Under pressure from her sisters, Julia agreed to let John live with the childless Mimi and her husband George Smith. She hope this would provide him with a more stable environment. He moved to Mendips, a semi-detached house in Menlove Avenue, Woolton, a pleasant middle-class suburb three miles outside Liverpool's city centre. George Smith was a respected man who owned the local farm and dairy. Julia knew that her son would be well looked after and that she would still see him most days.

John's artistic leanings emerged from birth. He was a bright child who had easily learned to read by the age of four. Mimi sent him off to school at Dovedale Primary, near Penny Lane. One of John's earliest passions was reading. He soon developed an interest in writing and drawing his own books and comics. He also began to develop a taste for the kind of petty mischief that would get him into trouble in the future.

At the age of 12 John was sent up to Quarry Bank Grammar, a school with a fine record of academic achievement. He started out as one the school's brightest hopes, but with his friend Pete Shotton always close at hand, John began a startling academic decline, increasingly creating trouble. Mimi, by now a widow, began to dread the phone calls from the school secretary detailing John's latest petty misdemeanours. By his early teens, John Lennon had already carved out a reputation as a rebel.

Whilst John worshipped Aunt Mimi, he had always remained very close to his mother. As he grew older he began to see more and more of her, often cutting out classes to do so. He thought of Julia more as an older sister than his mother. What's more, she told him the kind of things that he wanted to hear, like not to worry about homework or what might happen in the future. This was a contrast to Aunt Mimi, who was something of a disciplinarian.

Below Left: John Lennon as a child on a school trip to the Isle of Man.

Below Right: John Lennon's Ivor Novello award which he won with Paul McCartney for the song 'She's Leaving Home'.

"GROUPS WITH GUITARS ARE ON THEIR WAY OUT."

Dick Rowe, Head of Decca Records, infamously passed on The Beatles.

Right: November,1963 – Ringo Starr, George Harrison, Paul McCartney and John Lennon perform on *The Ken Dodd Show*.

WITH THE BEATLES

Label: Parlophone PCS 3045
Producer: George Martin
Release: November 22, 1963

SIDE ONE

IT WON'T BE LONG

(Lennon/McCartney)

Written and sung by John, 'It Won't Be Long' was intended as the follow up to 'She Loves You', but was rejected because it wasn't strong enough. In the context of the album however, the song makes a thoughtful opener.

ALL I'VE GOT TO DO

(Lennon/McCartney)

Another song written wholly by John. He later said it was an attempt to produce something that sounded like Smokey Robinson.

ALL MY LOVING

(Lennon/McCartney)

One of the most famous of The Beatles' early hits, 'All My Loving' was written and sung by Paul. It started life as a poem. As Paul says, "It was the first song I wrote where I had the words before the music.".

DON'T BOTHER ME

(Harrison)

Although George had been responsible for the occasional guitar instrumental, 'Don't Bother Me' was the first song he completed. It was put together in a hotel room in Bournemouth in August, where The Beatles were playing six concerts.

Left: The Beatles take a break from their Royal Variety Performance rehearsals at the Prince of Wales Theatre with a coffee at the Mapleton Hotel.

LITTLE CHILD

(Lennon/McCartney)

A joint composition that features Paul on piano and John on harmonica, with shared vocals, 'Little Child' seems to have been written primarily to give away to another artist.

TILL THERE WAS YOU

(Wilson)

Another show tune, this time written by Meredith Wilson for the show *Music Man*. Paul sings and plays bass, George and John play acoustic guitars, and Ringo joins in on the bongos. This is an unusually sparse arrangement for a beat group.

PLEASE MISTER POSTMAN

(Holland/Bateman/Gordy)

John's vocal is double-tracked on this version of the Marvelette's 1960 US million-selling debut single. The song was written by the Motown team of Brian Holland, Robert Bateman and owner Berry Gordy.

SIDE TWO

ROLL OVER BEETHOVEN

(Berry)

Chuck Berry was one of rock and roll's pioneers. He not only coined many of pop's best-known guitar licks, but he was a genuinely original lyricist. He was perhaps the first person to capture the spirit of teenage life in an intelligent or amusing way; ironic perhaps in that Berry himself was well into his thirties when he found fame. His classic 'Roll Over Beethoven' dates back to 1956, and had been in The Beatles' set before they even set foot in Hamburg. On the recorded version, George does the double-tracked vocal.

HOLD ME TIGHT

(Lennon/McCartney)

One of Paul's efforts that he regarded as a 'work song' – something knocked out for someone else to sing. It was a left-over from the first album, although newly recorded here. John by all accounts was not keen on this song. One

could easily imagine it being sung by popular girl groups of the time, such as the Shirelles or the Chiffons, whose hits they had covered so often.

YOU REALLY GOT A HOLD ON ME

(Robinson)

22-year-old William 'Smokey' Robinson was already a massive star in the US, with his hit group The Miracles, although they were relatively unknown in Europe. John and George share the lead vocal on 'You Really Got A Hold On Me', their second million-seller. John's early patronage of Smokey Robinson helped to pave the way for his many UK hits throughout the Sixties and Seventies.

I WANNA BE YOUR MAN

(Lennon/McCartney)

More closely associated with the Rolling Stones, cited throughout the 1960s as The Beatles' bitter rivals, although in truth they were good friends. The Stones' manager Andrew Oldham ran into John and Paul and asked if they had any new material that the Stones could use for a new single. They went into a studio where the Stones were rehearsing and played them a half-finished version of the song. The band liked it, so Lennon and McCartney disappeared off to finish it, emerging a few minutes later with the last verse and middle eight! Whilst it was a Top 20 hit for the Rolling Stones, The Beatles chose to let Ringo loose on their cut.

DEVIL IN HER HEART

(Drapkin)

George takes the lead vocal again on this track, a cover of a song by a relatively obscure US girl-group, the Donays. Ringo plays the maracas.

NOT A SECOND TIME

(Lennon/McCartney)

Written by John, who double-tracks the vocals, 'Not a Second Time' is another soul-influenced number. This led to William Mann, the music critic of *The Times*, writing an

Above: The Beatles proudly parade an assortment of silver discs presented by EMI records in London to mark sales of the LP *Please Please Me*.

over-enthusiastic article entitled 'What Songs The Beatles Sang'. He gushingly compares the track to Gustav Mahler's 'Song of the Earth', saying: "One gets the impression that they think simultaneously of harmony and melody, so firmly are the major tonic sevenths and ninths built into their tunes." He continues in this vein, going on to discuss the Aeolian cadence at the end of the song. John thought Aeolian cadences sounded "like exotic birds".

MONEY (THAT'S WHAT I WANT)

(Bradford/Gordy)

'Money' was originally recorded by Barrett Strong, and was Motown's first ever number one hit. John sings the album's closing number, and George Martin plays piano.

1964 THE AMERICAN DREAM

One might have thought that a contract with a major international record company like EMI would have opened doors – particularly as they already owned the powerful American Capitol label. But when George Martin sent a copy of *Please Please Me* to his opposite number at Capitol, the reaction was not positive.

The Beatles' American campaign began when Brian Epstein made his first visit to New York late in 1963. He called in on Brown Meggs, Director of Eastern Operations with Capitol Records, and played the demo of 'I Want to Hold Your Hand'. Capitol reluctantly agreed to give The Beatles a try. The ammunition for Brian's onslaught came from a less expected source. Ed Sullivan was a famous TV show host who had launched many celebrity careers, not least of all, Elvis. When he was caught up in a Beatlemania outburst between flights in London he saw no reason the boys couldn't elicit the same reaction in the US. He booked them for two shows in February 1964, hedging his bets by paying a tiny fee.

Capitol, meanwhile, were starting to do surprisingly well with 'I Want to Hold Your Hand'. On January 16, it leapt from number 43 to number one in the US Billboard charts. Radio stations who had got hold of the track were reporting huge listener interest. Capitol were bemused, but seized the opportunity – particularly with the impending Ed Sullivan appearance – and finally started a publicity blitz – the now-famous 'Beatles Are Coming' teaser campaign.

Beatles merchandise was being produced at this time by Nicky Byrne, a London socialite to whom Brian had naively given exclusive global merchandise rights for just ten per cent of the profit. However this may have ultimately been an advantage since Byrne was hugely motivated in helping The Beatles win over the US. He felt Capitol weren't doing enough, and quietly planned his own campaign. He printed 5,000 Beatles T-shirts, and prominently advertised them free – plus a $1 bill to boot – to any teen who went to greet The Beatles arriving at New York's newly named JFK airport.

Brian and The Beatles, who had no idea, were overwhelmed to disembark in America and discover the entire airport swarmed with an insane barrage of screaming fans, press packs, TV crews, and a hundred-strong police force trying to keep it all controlled. Suddenly all of America was very aware that The Beatles had landed.

Two days later, The Beatles played Ed Sullivan's show. It was watched on a jaw-dropping sixty per cent of American TV sets, breaking all previous records. To cap off the evening, Elvis Presley and his manager, Colonel Tom Parker, sent Ed Sullivan a telegram for The Beatles during the performance, passing on best wishes, welcomes, and congratulations.

America had succumbed completely. Nothing illustrates this surrender as clearly as the Billboard charts on April 4. The Beatles were occupying the top two positions on the album chart, and appeared in the singles chart, at numbers 1, 2, 3, 4, 5, 31, 41, 46, 58, 65, 68 and 79. No artist has ever come close to this level of domination, and it's difficult to imagine it ever happening again. For his part in whipping up American Beatlemania, Nicky Byrne made almost $100,000 profit – a huge sum at the time.

THE SILVER SCREEN

Such success brought about the opportunity of a cinema cash-in. Brian negotiated a three-film deal with United Artists. He was determined not to go below 7.5 per cent royalty: UA were happy to oblige – they had expected to pay 25 per cent! Brian was clearly getting out of his depth. Still, it wasn't as if the lads were short of cash. The Beatlemania fuss gave them a chance to relax the hectic tour schedule, and they took the time to make their first UA movie instead: *A Hard Day's Night*. Director Richard Lester and writer Alun Owen cleverly avoided putting too much pressure on The Beatles, instead giving them a series of fun set-pieces around London. The script was snappy, and the scenes close enough to the group's real lives for their performances to be convincing. The film became a huge hit, and earned Owen an Oscar.

1964 went on in a blur of global international tours, media appearances, plush hotel rooms and everywhere, *everywhere*, hordes of screaming fans. Holland, Sweden, Australia, Hong Kong, America again, a major British tour, and on and on and on. It started to get horrifying at times. George Martin commented: "In some places they'd wheel in paraplegics who were brought in to touch them – it was like Jesus, almost." The band's success was turning them into prisoners. By the end of the year, they were burnt out.

Above: The Beatles were greeted by thousands of screaming fans at Liverpool Airport (now Liverpool John Lennon Airport) as they returned from America.

Below: An (unused) ticket to the Hollywood Bowl, August 23, 1964.

Opposite: The Beatles take a dip. Ringo's not impressed.

Overleaf: Paul McCartney and John Lennon during on-stage rehearsals for the 1964 North American tour.

New Influences

Despite the harried year, a considerable development could be heard in some of The Beatles' new songs. While they were in America, the New York folk scene had thrown up the 'protest' song. The most prominent singer/songwriters of this new folk movement was the young Bob Dylan, his sparse acoustic albums providing anthems for a disaffected American youth. While on tour, The Beatles met Bob Dylan – it was here they were reputed to have first smoked marijuana. The whole of the band fell under the spell of Dylan's music.

Perhaps one of The Beatles greatest strengths was their open-mindedness when it came to new influences. In spite of the fact that they were now the most popular entertainers on the face of the planet, they were nonetheless happy to acknowledge that there were a lot of other interesting things worthy of checking out. As George later recalled: "We had Dylan's album and we played it over and over again – it gave us a real buzz." Paul was even more enthusiastic: "He was our idol."

It is not difficult to understand Dylan's appeal to such craftsmanlike songwriters as John Lennon and Paul McCartney. His lone acoustic guitar backing music allowed his powerful lyrics to do the talking. Until now, The Beatles had concerned themselves with developing their skills as musicians. The lesson that they, and countless others, learned from Bob Dylan was that it was possible to say something more than just the blindingly obvious or emotionally trite in the context of a pop song.

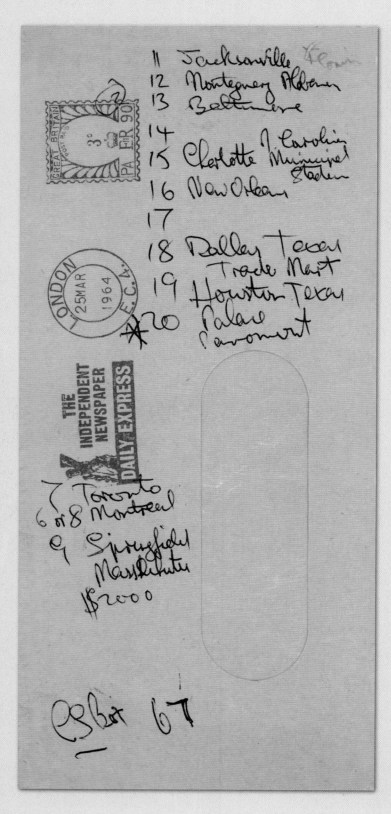

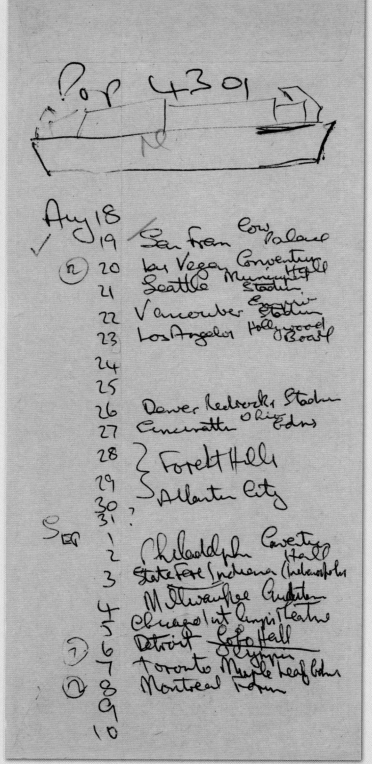

11 Jacksonville Floria
12 Montgomery Alabama
13 Baltimore
14 J Carolina
15 Charlotte Municipal Stadium
16 New Orleans
17
18 Dallas Texas Trade Mart
19 Houston Texas
*20 Palace Government

6 or 7 Toronto
or 8 Montreal
9 Springfield Massachusetts
$2000

Pop 4301

Aug 18
✓ 19 San Fran Cow Palace
Ⓡ 20 Las Vegas Convention Hall
21 Seattle Municipal Stadium
22 Vancouver Empire Stadium
23 Los Angeles Hollywood Bowl
24
25
26 Denver Redrocks Stadium
27 Cincinatti Ohio Gardens
28 } Forest Hills
29 } Atlantic City
30
31 ?
Sep 1
2 Philadelphia Convention Hall
3 State Fare Indiana (Indianapolis)
4 Milwaukee Auditorium
5 Chicago Int Amph Theatre
Ⓡ 6 Detroit Cobo Hall
7 Toronto Maple Leaf Gdns
Ⓡ 8 Montreal Forum
9
10

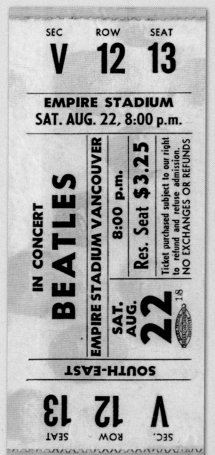

SEC **V** ROW **12** SEAT **13**

EMPIRE STADIUM
SAT. AUG. 22, 8:00 p.m.

IN CONCERT

BEATLES

EMPIRE STADIUM VANCOUVER

8:00 p.m.

Res. Seat $3.25

Ticket purchased subject to our right to refund and refuse admission. NO EXCHANGES OR REFUNDS

SAT. AUG. **22**
18

SOUTH-EAST

SOUVENIR PROGRAM

THE BEATLES

MANILA, PHILIPPINES
RIZAL MEMORIAL
FOOTBALL STADIUM
JULY 4, 1966

RIZAL MEMORIAL FOOTBALL STADIUM
MANILA

THE BEATLES

July 4, 1966 — 4:00 P.M.

THE BEATLES

₱20.00   Section BB

                Row 9

FIELD RESERVED   Seat 40

1501

Triangle Theatrical Productions

Franklin Fried
PRESENTS

THE BEATLES

Milwaukee Auditorium — Sept. 4 — Milwaukee

Above: Ticket for concert at Rizal Memorial Football Stadium, Manila, 1966, including the programme.

Right: Milwaukee Auditorium programme cover, 1964.

A HARD DAY'S NIGHT

Label: Parlophone PCS 2058
Producer: George Martin
Release: August 11, 1964

SIDE ONE

A HARD DAY'S NIGHT

(Lennon/McCartney)

From the distinctive chime of the Rickenbacker guitar in the opening chord, 'A Hard Day's Night' illustrates a continuing maturity in Lennon and McCartney's compositions. The song opened and closed the film, and was released as a single a month before the album. With advance orders of over half-a-million it became The Beatles' third consecutive single to enter the charts at number one. John wrote the song for his son Julian, who was about to celebrate his first birthday. *The Goon Show* star Peter Sellers also enjoyed a Top 20 hit with a comedy version of the song in 1965. His take was delivered music-free in the style of a Shakespearean monologue. Pianist Ramsey Lewis also scraped into the lower reaches of the Top 30 a year later with a jazz version.

I SHOULD HAVE KNOWN BETTER

(Lennon/McCartney)

John wrote, sang double-tracked vocals and played harmonica on this track. 'I Should Have Known Better' also features George playing a Rickenbacker 12-string guitar – he was largely responsible for the popularity of the instrument which was later taken up by American bands like the Byrds.

IF I FELL

(Lennon/McCartney)

In the film, there deliberately being no romantic interest for any of The Beatles, John sings this gentle love song to Ringo! The scene had to be shot a number of times as the band regularly broke down in fits of laughter.

"IN SOME PLACES THEY'D WHEEL IN PARAPLEGICS WHO WERE BROUGHT IN TO TOUCH THEM. IT WAS LIKE JESUS, ALMOST."

George Martin

I'M HAPPY JUST TO DANCE WITH YOU
(Lennon/McCartney)

Another of John's songs, although this time given to George to sing to allow him "a piece of the action".

AND I LOVE HER
(Lennon/McCartney)

It was generally assumed, although later denied, that Paul McCartney wrote 'And I Love Her' for his new girlfriend, actress Jane Asher. The recording is a completely acoustic one, with Ringo playing percussion. Unusually, given that it is an album track, this song is one of the most covered of all Beatles songs, with around 400 versions recorded.

TELL ME WHY
(Lennon/McCartney)

A throwaway up-tempo number written by John, again, with an American girl-group in mind. It was used during the concert sequence of the film.

CAN'T BUY ME LOVE
(Lennon/McCartney)

Primarily Paul's number, this was a late addition to the film. 'Can't Buy Me Love' was recorded in Paris, although George decided to overdub a 12-string Rickenbacker lead guitar part in London – the original solo is still audible in background. The track had already been released as a single in March, to the highest ever advance sales – over two million in the US and one million in the UK. Inevitably the single entered the charts at number one.

SIDE TWO

ANY TIME AT ALL
(Lennon/McCartney)

John Lennon has said that this track was a recycled version of 'It Won't Be Long' from their last album. He sings the lead, with Paul and George performing the backing vocal duties.

I'LL CRY INSTEAD
(Lennon/McCartney)

John originally wrote 'I'll Cry Instead' for the film, but director Richard Lester felt it was unsuitable for the scene he had in mind – a sequence involving a fire escape. 'Can't Buy Me Love' was used instead.

THINGS WE SAID TODAY
(Lennon/McCartney)

The flip side of the 'A Hard Day's Night' single, this was another of Paul's supposed love songs to Jane Asher. He wrote it on a yacht in the Caribbean during May, when all four Beatles took a month-long break after filming had ended.

WHEN I GET HOME
(Lennon/McCartney)

When John Lennon was asked what song he wished he could have written, his immediate reply was Marvin Gaye's 12-bar 'Can I Get A Witness'. 'When I Get Home' was John's attempt to write a similar style of song.

Above: A postcard from the filming of *Help!*, 1965.

Opposite: The Beatles escape from screaming fans in a still from *A Hard Day's Night*.

YOU CAN'T DO THAT
(Lennon/McCartney)

The flip side of 'Can't Buy Me Love' was recorded in Paris at the same time. John wrote the song and played lead on his new Rickenbacker guitar, while George played a 12-string guitar.

I'LL BE BACK
(Lennon/McCartney)

Written by John after Del Shannon's 'Runaway'. Shannon, who had enjoyed a spectacular career in the US, took a cover version of 'From Me To You' into the lower end of the American Top 100 charts before The Beatles ever managed to get there.

BEATLES FOR SALE

Label: Parlophone PCS 3062
Producer: George Martin
Release: December 4, 1964

SIDE ONE

NO REPLY

(Lennon/McCartney)

Lennon's 'No Reply' is based on a late 1950s American hit called 'Silhouettes' by the Rays. Along with 'Eight Days a Week', it was considered as a possible new single, until John came up with 'I Feel Fine'. Northern Songs publisher Dick James regarded it as Lennon's best song to date.

I'M A LOSER

(Lennon/McCartney)

John also wrote and sang this Dylan-influenced number. John has also claimed that this was the first of his songs to be influenced by the BBC interviewer Kenneth Allsop. Earlier in the year Lennon had published *In His Own Write*, a best-selling book of his drawings, poems and nonsense verse – it was much the same kind of thing that he had been doing for years since he was a child. Allsop encouraged Lennon to write more songs based on his own experiences and feelings rather than generalized emotions. 'I'm A Loser' is perhaps the first of Lennon's many future attempts at some kind of self-exploration.

BABY'S IN BLACK

(Lennon/McCartney)

Written by John and Paul, 'Baby's in Black' was the first song they had sat down to write together since 'I Want to Hold Your Hand'.

Left: The Beatles prepare for their Christmas show at the Hammersmith Palais.

ROCK AND ROLL MUSIC

(Berry)

One of Chuck Berry's best-loved songs, and a genuine classic, 'Rock and Roll Music' had been on their set list since their first days in Hamburg.

I'LL FOLLOW THE SUN

(Lennon/McCartney)

Written by Paul in 1959 after the death of his hero Buddy Holly. Holly had a major impact on The Beatles, being one of only a few pop stars of the period to write his own material. Indeed, McCartney was such a fan that in the 1970s he bought the publishing rights to all of Buddy Holly's songs. [Ironically, McCartney does not own the rights to his own Beatles songs. When they came up for sale in the 1980s they were bought up by his friend Michael Jackson. They fell out as a consequence!]

MR MOONLIGHT

(Jackson)

Written by Roy Lee Jackson, the song was originally recorded in 1962 by Dr Feelgood and the Interns. Although it was not a hit, several of the Merseybeat bands did their own versions. Here, John takes the lead vocal, Paul plays a Hammond organ and George plays an African drum.

KANSAS CITY

(Leiber/Stoller)

Although only credited as 'Kansas City' on the LP sleeve, it is in fact a medley that segues into Little Richard's 'Hey, Hey, Hey'. Paul sings the lead vocal, with John and George joining in at the end.

SIDE TWO

EIGHT DAYS A WEEK

(Lennon/McCartney)

Written by Paul and inspired by one of Ringo's descriptions of The Beatles' workload at the time. John and Paul share the lead vocals.

WORDS OF LOVE

(Holly)

John and Paul share the vocal on one of Buddy Holly's early singles, which flopped when it was originally released in 1957. Instead of playing the drums, Ringo taps out a rhythm on a packing case.

HONEY DON'T

(Perkins)

Carl Perkins was one of rock and roll's great pioneers, and is perhaps best remembered for writing 'Blue Suede Shoes', covered so memorably by Elvis Presley. With slightly less panache, Ringo takes the lead vocal here in his own inimitable style.

EVERY LITTLE THING

(Lennon/McCartney)

Written by Paul with some help from John. 'Every Little Thing' is a love song dedicated to Jane Asher.

I DON'T WANT TO SPOIL THE PARTY

(Lennon/McCartney)

John wrote the song and sings the lead vocal. It was written at a time when John was beginning to find it increasingly difficult to retain the lovable chirpy Beatle image when meeting people from the music industry.

WHAT YOU'RE DOING

(Lennon/McCartney)

A novel approach is on display here as the band shouts out the first word of each verse while Paul goes on to finish the line. It shows an attention to detail that would become an increasingly important element of subsequent recordings.

EVERYBODY'S TRYING TO BE MY BABY

(Perkins)

Another Carl Perkins song, this time sung by George Harrison. All three of the Perkins songs covered by The Beatles ('Matchbox' appeared only on the *Long Tall Sally* EP) were lifted from Perkins' 1958 Sun album *Teen Beat*.

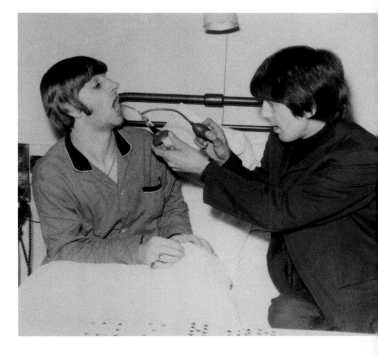

Above: Ringo Starr and George Harrison fool around at University College Hospital, London, while the drummer recovers from a tonsillectomy.

ADDITIONAL NOTES:

• *Beatles for Sale* was issued in America as *Beatles '65*. American albums of the time were usually shorter than their British counterparts, and the track listing differs substantially. Side one features only the first five tracks, while side two comprises 'Honey Don't', 'I'll Be Back' (an out-take from the film), 'She's a Woman' (the flip side of the new single), 'I Feel Fine' and 'Everybody's Trying To Be My Baby'. Of the unused tracks, 'Eight Days a Week' was a million-selling single in the US in 1965, and the remainders found their way onto the US-only *Beatles VI* album released six months later.

• An additional track, 'Leave My Kitten Alone' (a British beat group favourite written by 1950s American R&B performer Little Willie John), was also recorded for the album but never mixed. It appeared on many bootlegs over the years before finding a first official release in 1995 on the *Anthology 1* compilation CD set.

George Harrison Ringo Starr Paul McCartney

John Lennon

"THEY WERE SOMEWHAT ILL-CLAD AND THE PRESENTATION LEFT A LOT TO BE DESIRED."

Brian Epstein, on seeing The Beatles for the first time.

Left: A still from The Beatles' movie debut, *A Hard Day's Night*, released on August 11, 1964.

PAUL MCCARTNEY

James Paul McCartney was born in Liverpool's Walton General Hospital on June 18, 1942. His father Jim, like many "Scousers", had an Irish background. He worked during the day on the Liverpool Cotton Exchange in Chapel Street, before the war forced its closure. At night, however, he turned to his first love – music. Jim was a self-taught pianist who led the Jim Mac Jazz Band, making an extra few shillings playing at social clubs and works dances. Whilst Jim McCartney had a reputation as a diligent and skilful salesman, he was also by all accounts something of ladies' man. Having successfully escaped the responsibility of marriage and a family throughout his twenties and thirties, he seemed destined for a life of bachelorhood. Then he met Mary Mohan. They married in 1941, a few months before Jim's 40th birthday.

Paul was seemingly graced from birth with charm that would get him out of all manner of childhood scrapes. Performing well at primary school, Paul easily passed his Eleven Plus examinations, winning a place at the City's most prestigious grammar school, The Liverpool Institute. Paul was a model pupil, always helpful and quietly studious. He held his own easily in the school's A-stream, finding that most schoolwork came to him quite easily. In subjects that he didn't enjoy he could still usually muster enough effort to achieve at least a low-grade pass.

Paul's grandfather, Joe McCartney, was strictly traditional about his musical tastes. He enjoyed opera and brass bands, and played the double bass in the house, and the tuba for two separate bands – a local Territorial Army band, based out of Stanley Park, and the house band of the Tobacco factory where he worked. He had always been hopeful of interesting his children in the musical arts. Jim irritated his father by turning to ragtime music at the age of 17, having learnt by ear to play both the piano and the trumpet. Joe had little time for Jim's choice of musical style, but that didn't stop Paul's father. Jim first appeared in public with a band called the Masked Melody

Makers who were remembered for wearing black masks on stage. Jim later put together Jim Mac's Jazz Band, which included his brother Jack, who played trombone. Jim's first composition was a song called 'Eloise', to which Paul would later add lyrics and, as a tribute to his father, record in the mid-1970s as 'Walking in the Park with Eloise'.

In 1955, when Paul was still only 13, his mother fell ill. After experiencing pains in her chest she was diagnosed as having breast cancer. By the time she was taken into hospital for exploratory surgery, the cancer had already spread too far and the proposed mastectomy operation could not be performed. Mary died shortly afterwards. Devastated by her death, Jim took over the arduous task of looking after the family finances – Mary's wages as a health worker had always been relied upon to keep their heads above water – and rearing Paul and Michael, his two teenage sons.

With a musician for a father, the McCartney household had always been filled with music. Like many homes before the arrival of television, the family's upright piano – purchased coincidentally from Brian Epstein's father, Harry, at the NEMS shop – was the centre-piece around which the family would

Above: The Beatles in Hamburg, 1962. Photograph by Astrid Kirchherr.

Right: Paul McCartney with father, Jim and brother, Mike.

"I REMEMBER GETTING HOME TO ENGLAND AND MY DAD THOUGHT I WAS HALF-DEAD."

Paul, upon returning home from Hamburg, 1961.

congregate for communal sing-songs. But the McCartneys were now distinctly out of tune with each other. Jim had already bought a nickel-plated trumpet for Paul's birthday following Mary's death. Like John Lennon, however, Paul had also heard Lonnie Donegan and wanted to play a guitar. While Jim McCartney had displayed an interest in the new rock and roll music, he was more concerned that his family should not have a Teddy Boy in their number. He was also largely unconvinced of the merits of the guitar as a musical instrument.

Eventually, without too much persuasion – and quite possibly remembering his own childhood and his musical disagreements with his father – Jim relented. One day he took the trumpet out with him to work, and came home having exchanged it for a sunburst-coloured guitar. He set about teaching Paul some basic chords. However, he was surprised to see the difficulty with which Paul squeezed the fingers of his left hand into position on the fret board. Paul struggled for a while before giving up completely. Until, that is, the day he discovered that by holding the guitar in the other hand the whole process was somehow much simpler. This was rather strange: whilst Paul McCartney was right-handed in every other way, for some mysterious reason, playing guitar right-handed felt completely wrong. After restringing the guitar, Paul set about learning the chords once again. This time there was no turning back.

From that moment on. Paul devoted all his waking hours to the instrument, and – like generations of others before and since – a promising start to an academic career was cut short by the lure of the six-stringed beast.

Left: Six-year-old Paul McCartney with younger brother Mike, 1948.

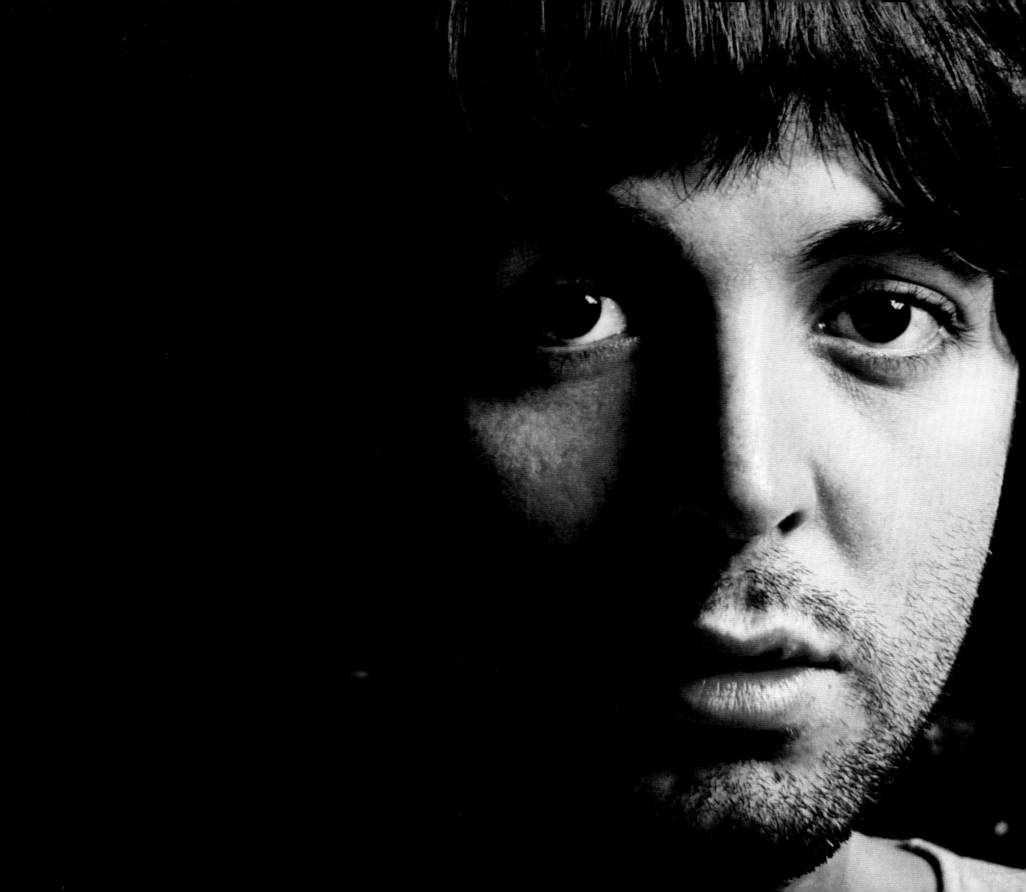

1965 TRANSFORMATION

If 1964 was the year in which The Beatles took on the whole world, 1965 was to be their year of transition. Although they were still fantastically popular, the Beatlemania phenomenon was beginning to show signs of running out of steam. While the great wheels of Brian Epstein's NEMS empire were grinding relentlessly onwards, the four young men at the sharp end were beginning to have ideas of their own. In private, they all agreed that some major changes were needed.

Life as a Beatle was intolerable. The band wanted to cut down on the amount of time devoted to touring and transfer their energies into songwriting and mastering the recording process. If 1964 marked The Beatles as the most potent commercial force in music history, then 1965 sowed the seeds of a transformation that would see The Beatles change the course of popular music.

January kicked off exactly as the last year had finished – more exhausting performances. The following month The Beatles attempted to resume their normal family lives – as if such a thing, as a Beatle, were possible. John went back to his surrey Mansion, Kenwood, and settled into family life with Cynthia and Julian. Paul was gadding around the London social scene with Jane Asher, a pretty young actress and socialite. George had his own Surrey estate, Kinfauns, where he lived with model Patti Boyd, who he'd met whilst filming *A Hard Day's Night*. Ringo meanwhile was involved with local Liverpool hairdresser Maureen Cox, who he'd snagged out of the queue for the Cavern one night. When word of their relationship came to light, she received the full jealous venom of Liverpool's teenage girls.

On February 15, The Beatles resumed recording at Abbey Road studios and – luxury of luxuries – were given a whole week to do the soundtrack for their upcoming second film. *Help!* would be shot in the Caribbean and other exotic locations, but whilst Richard Lester was back at the helm in the director's chair, the script came from American comedy writer Marc Behm. He was well respected, but failed to capture the band's spirit and essential Englishness. The film was a great financial success of course, but received far less critical acclaim than *A Hard Day's Night*. The band themselves hated it.

After filming, the group returned to the studio to record some more songs for the second side of the soundtrack album, and which didn't feature in the film. On Monday,

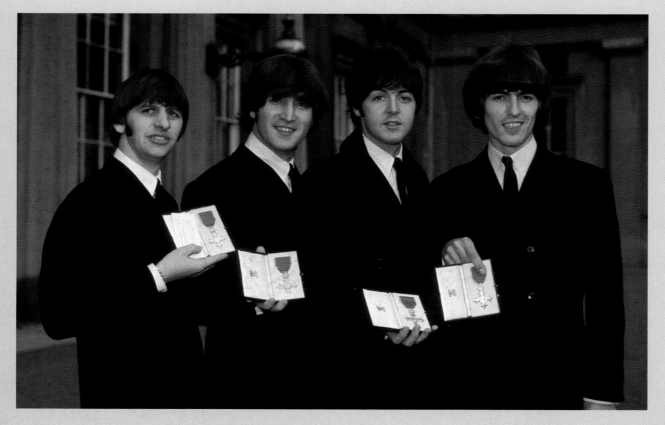

June 14, Paul McCartney started the recording of a song on which he'd been working for some time. 'Yesterday' has become one of the most recorded songs of the past 40 years. It wasn't released as a single at the time, however. By the end of July, 'Help!' the single, *Help!* the album and *Help!* the film were all unleashed on the public. All three went straight to the top of their respective charts.

ESTABLISHMENT

Only days after the premiere of *Help!* The Beatles hit America for a third time. Sunday, August 15 saw their momentous concert at the home of the Mets baseball team in New York City. It was the absolute pinnacle of The Beatles as public performers. The crowd of 55,600 fans was the largest ever for a pop concert, the box office

receipts the highest of all time, and so too The Beatles' own takings – $160,000.

The rest of the tour lacked the sparkle of the opening triumph and the band quickly lost interest. Moreover, they had actively begun to hate being on tour. They had a six-week break afterwards, but Lennon and McCartney were obliged to use their time to produce material for a new album. Yet despite the pressure of coming up with twelve songs in six weeks, *Rubber Soul* turned out to be a surprisingly strong transitional album.

Back in the UK, news broke that The Beatles were to be honoured with MBEs by the Queen. A furore ensued, and some former MBEs returned their medals in protest. The press, however, were ecstatic. John was less keen until Brian persuaded him that accepting would be a beneficial move. Brian himself was overlooked. Depressed, he took it as a personal snub, believing it to be because he was both Jewish and homosexual.

The investiture ceremony took place at Buckingham Palace on October 26. Outside, 4,000 screaming fans were held back by a heavy police cordon, chanting "Long Live The Queen! Long Live The Beatles!" During the ceremony, and at the press conference afterwards, The Beatles kept up their quirky humour. Outside, waving their silver crosses in front of the assembled press Paul told them that the Queen was, "… lovely, great. She was very friendly. She was like a mum to us," and that Buckingham Palace was a "keen pad".

The year ended in an unsurprising style for the group, with *Rubber Soul* shooting straight to the top of the album charts, and a groundbreaking double 'A'-side single – 'Day Tripper'/'We Can Work It Out' – dominating the world's singles charts.

Opposite: The Beatles outside Buckingham Palace, after receiving their MBEs.

Left: Ticket for the June 20 show at the Palais des Sports, Paris.

Above: The Beatles at Cliveden during the filming of *Help!*.

HELP!

Label: Parlophone PCS 3071
Producer: George Martin
Release: August 6, 1965

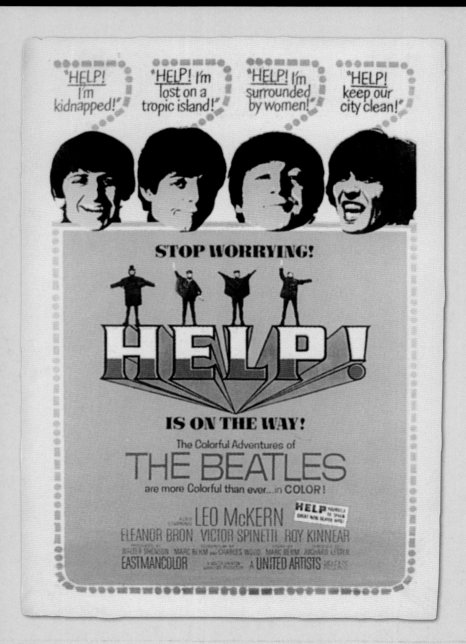

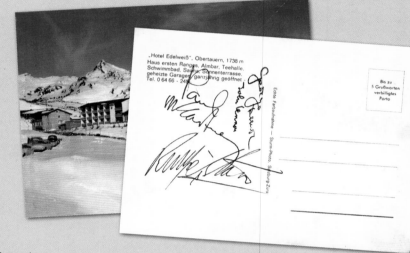

SIDE ONE

HELP!

(Lennon/McCartney)

One of John Lennon's personal favourites, it was originally written as a slow, Dylanesque acoustic number and he later went on record saying that he regretted how the song had been "Beatlefied". In spite of the misgivings of the composer, 'Help!' remains one of the Beatle's most popular songs and features some of Lennon's most deeply felt and personal lyrics. Reflecting his increasing dissatisfaction with himself and his life, Lennon confirmed: "It was real … it was me singing 'Help!' and I meant it … I needed the help." He also added one other footnote: "I don't like the recording much – we did it too fast, trying to be commercial."

THE NIGHT BEFORE

(Lennon/McCartney)

Written by Paul, the song is performed in the film with the band surrounded by tanks and soldiers on Salisbury Plain. John plays the electric piano. The *Help!* album showed that the imbalance between Lennon and McCartney as songwriters was showing signs of levelling out.

Above: Signed postcard from *Help!* filming, 1965.

Left: Poster advertising *Help!* the movie.

Right: George Harrison, Paul McCartney and John Lennon photographed during the filming of *Help!*.

YOU'VE GOT TO HIDE YOUR LOVE AWAY

(Lennon/McCartney)

Another very personal song about which John later said: "When I was a teenager I used to write poetry, but was always trying to hide my real feelings … instead of projecting myself into a situation I would just try to express what I felt about myself … I think it was Dylan that helped me realize that."

I NEED YOU

(Harrison)

Written by George – his second writing contribution to The Beatles – 'I Need You' shows a developing confidence, but that his songwriting still lacked the sophistication of the other two writers in the band.

ANOTHER GIRL

(Lennon/McCartney)

Paul wrote and sang 'Another Girl'. Paul was always considered to be the natural musician of the band. Here, keen to display his fast-growing talents, he also plays lead guitar. John and George provide backing vocals.

YOU'RE GOING TO LOSE THAT GIRL

(Lennon/McCartney)

John makes a threat that if "you" continue to mistreat your girlfriend he's ready to make a move on her himself.

TICKET TO RIDE

(Lennon/McCartney)

Already a million-selling single by the time *Help!* was shown, John wrote the song and rated it among his personal favourites. Paul takes the lead guitar again.

SIDE TWO

ACT NATURALLY

(Morrison/Russell)

A Beatles album wouldn't have been the same without Ringo taking the microphone for the occasional song. 'Act Naturally' was a novelty country and western hit for Buck Owens in America.

IT'S ONLY LOVE

(Lennon/McCartney)

At a time when his lyrical ideas were becoming increasingly sophisticated, John Lennon also showed how he could turn out the laziest of clichéd rhyming couplets as easily as any old Tin Pan Alley hack. Later he would confess: "I was always ashamed of that because of the abominable lyrics." Oddly, however, a cover of 'It's Only Love', recorded by Gary US Bonds, scraped into the nether regions of the charts as recently as 1981. We can only guess why.

YOU LIKE ME TOO MUCH

(Harrison)

One of nine demos originally handed to Richard Lester for the film, 'You Like Me Too Much' was eventually recorded for side two of the album. When George published his autobiography *I Me Mine* in 1980, he made no mention of either of his contributions to the *Help!* album. This is perhaps because, whilst within a few years he would be come a more than capable composer in his own right, the tracks presented here show him feeling his way, but still well and truly in the shadow of his two senior colleagues.

TELL ME WHAT YOU SEE

(Lennon/McCartney)

One of Paul's lazier efforts, 'Tell Me What You See' was also rejected from the *Help!* soundtrack. The composer of the song even has his doubts about the track's composition, 'I seem to remember it is as mine … not awfully memorable,' McCartney admitted in an interview years later. Despite this, the song highlights McCartney's growth as a songwriter since his compositions on *A Hard Day's Night*.

I'VE JUST SEEN A FACE

(Lennon/ McCartney)

Paul had been playing this tune on the piano for some time back in Liverpool. His Aunt Gin was so taken with the melody that it became known as 'Auntie Gin's Theme'.

YESTERDAY

(Lennon McCartney)

One of the most famous songs in pop history, and one of Paul

McCartney's finest moments. Within ten years 'Yesterday' had been recorded by 1,186 other artists – the figure is now likely to be well over 2,000. In a 1999 BBC poll, listeners voted 'Yesterday' the best song of the 20th century.

DIZZY MISS LIZZY

(Williams)

When in doubt, The Beatles would always return to their origins. 'Dizzy Miss Lizzy' was another rock and roll classic they had been performing since the Kaiserkeller days in Hamburg. The Beatles performed several songs by its American author, Larry Williams, whose principal success came in 1958 with the million-seller 'Bony Moronie'.

ADDITIONAL NOTES

• On the British pressing of *Help!* only the songs on the first side can actually be heard in the film. The American pressing features only these six songs interspersed with orchestral versions or some of musical director Ken Thorne's incidental compositions.

• 'I've Just Seen a Face' and 'It's Only Love' appear on the US version of the later *Rubber Soul* album.

• 'Yesterday' and 'Act Naturally' appear on the US-only compilation album, *Yesterday and Today*.

RUBBER SOUL

Label: Parlophone PCS 3075
Producer: George Martin
Release: December 3, 1965

SIDE ONE

DRIVE MY CAR
(Lennon/McCartney)
This was one of John and Paul's increasingly rare joint efforts. In an amusing reversal of regular roles, the lyric tells the story of the possible favours that might result if the man in the song becomes "her" chauffeur. The chorus also features the famous "Beep-beep, beep-beep, yeah" backing vocals that have accompanied many a radio traffic broadcast ever since.

NORWEGIAN WOOD
(Lennon/McCartney)
'Norwegian Wood' was, by John's own admission, an attempt to confess that he had been unfaithful to Cynthia without actually telling her directly. John was not happy in his marriage and was known to have taken advantage of the numerous groupies and hangers-on that inevitably follow a successful band. The track is also notable for being the first use of the Indian sitar on a pop record. George had become interested in the instrument when one was used as a prop during the filming of *Help!*.

YOU WON'T SEE ME
(Lennon/McCartney)
Paul seemingly writing about a crisis in his relationship with Jane Asher, which was beginning to look decidedly shaky. Paul plays piano and long-term friend and road manager Mal Evans plays the Hammond organ.

Left: The Beatles performing at the *NME* Poll-Winners concert, 1965

NOWHERE MAN
(Lennon/McCartney)

In John's own words, "I was just sitting, trying to think of a song. And I thought of myself sitting there, doing nothing, and getting nowhere … sitting in this nowhere land." This was a departure in that up to that point every Beatles song had, to some extent, been about love.

THINK FOR YOURSELF
(Harrison)

George's best composition to date, featuring an unusual fuzz bass line courtesy of Paul.

THE WORD
(Lennon/McCartney)

The influence of LSD was now beginning to permeate John's work. This time, as it would so often in the future, it resulted in a calling for universal love and peace. He later described the song as The Beatles' first "message" song.

SIDE TWO

MICHELLE
(Lennon/McCartney)

Following the most startling song on the album, Paul's 'Michelle' comes across as a pretty, if rather trite, love song. For the French lyrics he contacted Ivan Vaughan – the school friend responsible for introducing him to John Lennon. Ivan was now married to a French language teacher. She provided him with "sont les mots qui vont tres bien ensemble", a translation of the previous line, "these are words that go together very well".

'Michelle' is probably the most famous song on the album, and versions by the Sandpipers and British duo David and Jonathan both had chart success. David and Jonathan were really Roger Cook and Roger Greenaway, who would become two of Britain's most prolific and successful songwriters of the 1970s.

WHAT GOES ON
(Lennon/McCartney/Starkey)

Ringo's first compositional credit: "I used to wish that I could write songs like the others – and I've tried, but I just can't." He later admitted that his input to the track was "about five words". Ringo also takes the lead vocal.

GIRL
(Lennon/McCartney)

At one time John said, "This was about a dream girl." Later however, perhaps ironically, he claimed he "was trying to say something about Christianity". Religion was a subject that increasingly concerned him at the time – as the "bigger than Jesus" controversy would soon show. As an additional boys' joke, the backing vocals feature Paul and George repeating the word "tit".

I'M LOOKING THROUGH YOU
(Lennon/McCartney)

With Jane Asher refusing to sacrifice her acting career to be the good little Beatle-wife, Paul was placed in a dilemma – one that was having an obvious affect on his lyric writing. 'I'm Looking Through You' is a bitter attack on a woman who seems to have changed, and he threatens that his love can disappear as easily as it arrived.

IN MY LIFE
(Lennon/McCartney)

In John's view, 'In My Life' was The Beatles' "first real major piece of work". One of John's most poignant sets of lyrics started life as a free-form poem that looked back nostalgically on some of the landmarks he remembered as a child, all of which were gradually disappearing or changing beyond his recognition. After losing the specific references 'In My Life' becomes a lament to the inevitable losses and changes that are outside of our control.

The source of the tune remains something of a minor controversy: John maintained that he wrote it with a little help from Paul; on the other hand, Paul recalls having written the whole tune himself.

WAIT
(Lennon/McCartney)

Jointly written by John and Paul, 'Wait' was recorded for *Help!* but not used. It was only resurrected for *Rubber Soul* because they were a song short.

IF I NEEDED SOMEONE
(Harrison)

Along with Bob Dylan, the Byrds – an American band that had taken electric guitars to folk music – were another growing influence on The Beatles. George's 'If I Needed Someone' was inspired by two Byrds' numbers – 'She Don't Care about Time' and 'The Bells of Rhymney'. The Hollies became the first band to cover one of George's songs when they took 'If I Needed Someone' into the Top 30. George's response to such an honour was a public declaration that he didn't much like their version!

RUN FOR YOUR LIFE
(Lennon/McCartney)

"I always hated 'Run For Your Life'" John said about the album's closing track. He openly acknowledged that he lifted two lines from Arthur Gunther's 'Baby Let's Play House', an early hit for Elvis Presley during his time recording for the Sun label in the mid-Fifties.

ADDITIONAL NOTES:
• Each side of the American version of *Rubber Soul* opens with a track from *Help!* – 'I've Just Seen a Face' and 'It's Only Love'. 'Drive My Car', 'Nowhere Man', 'What Goes On' and 'If I Needed Someone' do not appear on the album.

1966 ENOUGH IS ENOUGH

For the first three months of 1966 it was all quiet on the Beatle front. Indeed it was not until May that they actually played live again — by far their longest break since the days of the Quarrymen. The Beatles stepped back into their 'ordinary' lives. On April 6 they once again congregated at Abbey Road to begin work on album number seven. This time they worked solidly in the studio for almost three months — an unheard of extravagance in those days. *Revolver* was the stunning result.

Things, however, started to go awry in June. Their American label, Capitol, had planned to issue a compilation album, *Yesterday and Today*. This would contain album tracks that were not used on the US pressings of *Help!*, *Rubber Soul* and *Revolver*. All of their US albums up to this point had been scaled down versions of their British counterparts. On the early albums, this had been seen as just profiteering. However, *Revolver* and *Rubber Soul* seemed to be more like self-contained pieces of work. By chopping them up, Capitol became an uninvited artistic editor. The band were starting to get irritated but they were powerless to act. Yet they had no idea of the chaos that was currently ensuing at Capitol headquarters.

Yesterday and Today was slated to appear in a sleeve created, at The Beatles' request, by British photographer Robert Whitaker. The scene depicted the Fab Four with huge grins on their faces, wearing white butcher's smocks and covered in slabs of raw meat and mutilated dolls. A week before the album's release, Capitol was inundated with complaints about the potentially offensive nature of this photograph. After an emergency meeting Capitol decided that it should be withdrawn. Label staff spent the week prior to its release replacing the sleeve with a bland image. The fiasco cost Capitol Records $200,000.

THE PHILIPPINES ADVENTURE

July turned out to be similarly eventful. After three horrible, near-imprisoned days in Japan, the band moved on to the Philippines. Local media there had made a huge fuss about President Marcos and his wife Imelda meeting the group the morning after their first show. No-one had told the band though. When the presidential official came to collect them he discovered them still asleep and incommunicado.

In almost no time at all, the Philippine press had whipped the population into a nationalist frenzy over the 'insult'. The hotel and British embassy received bomb threats, the promoter refused to pay their share of the concert profits, their

Strawberry Fields Forever

The Beatles spent the last month of 1966 working almost entirely on a single track, John's nostalgic paean to Strawberry Field, a Salvation Army children's home around the corner from where he'd grown up. As the most complex recording The Beatles would ever make, 'Strawberry Fields Forever' called on George Martin to scale new heights of ingenuity with his armoury of production talents. The song had started out as a simple acoustic ballad, but as the group arrangement evolved, it took on a heavier tone, which John, eyeing from afar the activities of some of the new Californian groups, particularly liked. The Beatles recorded 26 different takes, from group versions to orchestral arrangements to experimental takes, and George Martin manage to somehow fulfil John's requests to distil them all down to a timeless, complex, multi-layered classic. The single was issued on February 17, 1967 backed by Paul's 'Penny Lane' — another Beatles classic. Critics were quick to hail both songs, but over the years 'Strawberry Fields Forever' has grown and grown to achieve legendary status. In the eyes of many, it is the greatest seven inches of vinyl ever produced. When viewed in conjunction with the short promotional film that was shot later in the year — an early video, in effect — the impact remains electrifying. Never has there been a set of images that so concisely evoked an era.

---

security abandoned them to violent crowds, and government departments fell over each other to harass the group with dubious legislative requirements.

Eventually, it cost Brian a load of 'fees' and 'fines' – and some minor injuries – before the band could even get to the airport. Even then, customs officials tried to frame them as illegal immigrants. By the time The Beatles finally managed to get out of the country, they were heartily sick of Asia. They got home with a couple of weeks to relax before heading off to America again.

A MATTER OF CONTEXT

The press have always been skilled at taking celebrity quotes out of context to create sensational headlines. Earlier in 1966, John had given an interview to the *Evening Standard*. In it, he talked openly about his interest in religion, adding that: "Christianity will go. It will vanish and shrink. I needn't argue with that … We're more popular than Jesus now."

No-one batted an eyelid until a US teen magazine published parts of the interview with the headline: "I don't know which will go first – rock and roll or Christianity." The American Bible Belt erupted. Radio stations nationwide banned The Beatles altogether, even holding numerous well-reported record-burnings events.

When The Beatles arrived in August, they were forced to immediately hold a press conference. John patiently explained to the media several times what he had actually meant, but all the pack wanted to know was whether he was prepared to retract what they had decided he'd said. John gracefully did his best to hide his bemusement and apologized, and the whole matter more or less vanished again. Any hint of enthusiasm the band had felt for the tour had been killed though, and they forced their way through. The final performance at Candlestick Park in San Francisco, on August 29, was notably only for one thing – it was to prove the last time that The Beatles ever performed on stage.

When The Beatles returned to London from America, everyone, Brian included, knew that things were going to be different from now on. They made no immediate plans to record again for three months.

In the mean time, John lent himself to some indifferent film work on Richard Lester's less than successful *How I Won The War*. Paul leapt into the London art scene. George went to India with Patti, taking sitar tuition from the great Ravi Shankar, and also immersing himself in spiritual instruction. Ringo was the only one who seemed relatively content with his lot, spending time with Maureen and his new son, Zak.

Opposite: The Beatles and their manager Brian Epstein arrive back in London from Manila after touring Germany, Japan and the Philippines.

Above: At a Chicago news conference John Lennon gives an apology for his remark that the Beatles were "more popular than Jesus".

Left: The Beatles perform at New York's Shea Stadium before a crowd of 45,000 people, August 23 1966.

REVOLVER

Label: Parlophone PCS 7009
Producer: George Martin
Release: August 5, 1966

SIDE ONE

TAXMAN

(Harrison)

Revolver showed the world that The Beatles now had a third highly capable songwriter in their midst. 'Taxman' was written when George, by now in the highest possible income tax bracket, found out how much of his earnings were taken in tax payments by the British government. George sings (as the tax collector): "There's one for you, nineteen for me". In pre-decimal currency, one pound was made up of 20 shillings. For every pound The Beatles earned in the highest tax bracket, they paid 19 shillings and three pence (96p) in income tax.

ELEANOR RIGBY

(Lennon/McCartney)

Revolver was also the first album where Paul could be said to have matched John's output. Released as a double "A" side single (backed by 'Yellow Submarine') on the same day as the album, Paul's 'Eleanor Rigby' is a simple story of loneliness. The main character came to Paul when he passed a wine merchant called Rigby and Evens while visiting Jane Asher, at the time performing in theatre in Bristol. It was later discovered that a woman of the same name had been buried in 1939 at St Peter's Church in Woolton, the backdrop for John and Paul's first meeting in 1957. The name may well have lurked in the depths of Paul's mind over the years. As he later said: "I was looking for a name that was natural. Eleanor Rigby sounded natural." George Martin's sophisticated baroque string quartet arrangement, creates an air of melancholy desperation that transforms the song into one of the most haunting records to ever grace the top of the hit parade.

Left: The Beatles study the streets below, 1966.

I'M ONLY SLEEPING

(Lennon/McCartney)

Maureen Cleave, in her notorious 'more popular than Jesus' *Evening Standard* piece earlier in the year, had already noted that John Lennon was now "probably the laziest person in England". This is illustrated perfectly in his first song for *Revolver*. The lazily strummed acoustic guitars and chorus melody lagging behind the beat perfectly evoke such a sensation. Although George Martin had used tape effects before (for example, speeding up the piano solo during *Rubber Soul*'s 'In My Life'), 'I'm Only Sleeping' features a backwards guitar solo. This was achieved by turning the audio tape around, recording the solo, and then playing it back the correct way again. This would become something of standard technique on many psychedelic recordings of the late 1960s.

LOVE YOU TO

(Harrison)

George's second contribution to the album showcases his continued interest in Indian music. George himself plays the sitar, while Indian musician Anil Bhagwat plays the tabla.

HERE, THERE AND EVERYWHERE

(Lennon/McCartney)

Thought by many to be Paul McCartney's finest love song. It was, again, inspired by his relationship with Jane Asher, which now looked to be back on course. It also took into account a new influence on the band – the Beach Boys. Like The Beatles, they were in the process of transforming themselves, and in the form of the fragile Brian Wilson, they also had a composer possessed of equal stature. Paul was especially impressed by the complex harmonic structure of 'God Only Knows' from the classic *Pet Sounds* album. 'Here, There and Everywhere' was an attempt to capture the same kind of atmosphere. Shortly before his death in 1980, John Lennon would declare that it was his favourite song The Beatles ever recorded.

YELLOW SUBMARINE

(Lennon/McCartney)

While many have attempted to furnish it with some mystic or drug-related meaning, Paul's 'Yellow Submarine', sung by Ringo, was simply intended to be a children's song. As such, as Paul says, it had to be: "Very easy … there isn't a single big word." 'Yellow Submarine' appeared on the flip side of 'Eleanor Rigby', providing the sharpest possible contrast, and evidence of The Beatles newfound freedom to please themselves.

SHE SAID SHE SAID

(Lennon/McCartney)

John's 'She Said She Said' is another evident sign of his growing use of LSD. The song came about following an organized acid trip the year before in San Diego with various members of the Byrds and actor Peter Fonda – who would find fame a few years later in the archetypal 1960s drug movie *Easy Rider*. Fonda remembers: "[Lennon] heard me say 'I know what it's like to be dead.' He looked at me and said 'You're making me feel I've never been born.'"

SIDE TWO

GOOD DAY SUNSHINE

(Lennon/McCartney)

Written by Paul and influenced by another popular American group of the time, the Lovin' Spoonful, who were themselves enjoying their first hit in Britain – 'Daydream' – while The Beatles were recording *Revolver*. Later, John Sebastian, leader of the Spoonful, would admit that it was seeing The Beatles on the *Ed Sullivan Show* that had given him the inspiration to form a group.

AND YOUR BIRD CAN SING

(Lennon/McCartney)

Although it features some inspired multi-tracked guitar playing by George, John surprisingly dismissed 'And Your Bird Can Sing' a number of times in later years. Although it is one of the highlights of this great album, he clearly felt that the song was an insubstantial piece of padding.

FOR NO ONE

(Lennon/McCartney)

Paul's 'For No One' is a poignant flashback to the point where a relationship is about to end. While John Lennon had all but stopped writing about such things, Paul McCartney had quietly become a master at detailing difficult emotional issues in a simple and coherent manner.

DR ROBERT

(Lennon/McCartney)

When asked to identify Dr Robert, Paul replied: "Well, he's like a joke. There's some fellow in New York … we'd hear people say, 'You can get everything off him; any pills you want' … [He] cured everyone of everything with these pills and tranquilizers … he just kept New York high."

The true identity of Dr Robert was most likely to have been Dr Robert Freymann, who had a practice on New York's East 78th Street. Many of his clients worked in the fields of art and entertainment: one of them was John Lennon, who wrote the song. Freymann was struck off in 1975, having been found guilty of malpractice.

I WANT TO TELL YOU

(Harrison)

The third of George's hat-trick of fine contributions to *Revolver*, 'I Want to Tell You' is an attempt to describe the frustration of being unable to articulate your thoughts – another phenomenon associated with the use of acid.

GOT TO GET YOU INTO MY LIFE

(Lennon/McCartney)

"We were influenced by our Tamla Motown bit on this." John was happy to continue his admission: "You see, we're influenced by whatever's going." In fact it was Paul who wrote the song and had the idea of adding a four-piece brass section.

TOMORROW NEVER KNOWS

(Lennon/McCartney)

Although 'Tomorrow Never Knows' is the final track, seemingly pointing to a future direction the band might take, it was the first song they recorded for the session. Originally referred to as 'The Void', after a line by the acid guru Timothy Leary, 'Tomorrow Never Knows' was a plain and simple effort by John Lennon to attempt to capture in sound the sensation of an acid trip. The song revolves around a raga-type repetitive rhythm – only two chords are used are used in the song – layered with 16 loops of randomly found sounds. John's original idea was that his vocal should be hidden among voices that sounded like a chorus of Tibetan monks chanting on a mountain-top.

1967 A FATAL BLOW

The new year kicked off with The Beatles still locked into the studio. In fact, right up until Friday, April 21 they virtually had a free run of Studio 2 at Abbey Road. Throughout this time they worked and reworked the same material with meticulous precision, ending up with what is arguably the most influential album in the history of popular music – *Sgt. Pepper's Lonely Hearts Club Band*. So much has been written about this album in the past 40 years that, like The Beatles themselves, it is difficult to review the work with any objectivity. Its musical and cultural significance simply shoot off the scale.

As was heard on *Revolver*, the Lennon/McCartney team were still pulling in very different directions. John's desire to experiment with sound made huge demands on George Martin, and helped to create a whole new genre of psychedelic music. In contrast, Paul's work was more straightforward, and his musicianship shines through track after track. *Sgt. Pepper* was received, by the public and critics alike, as no other record before. It topped the charts all over the world, and still receives massive attention and re-evaluation every time a notable release anniversary comes around.

THE DEATH OF BRIAN

In his element organizing the minutia of The Beatles' working lives during the past five years – and still only in his early 30s – Brian was beginning to feel like an unnecessary part of a machine. While The Beatles unquestionably loved and respected him, they now had firm opinions of their own. As George Martin said during the *Sgt. Pepper* recordings: "When John had finished singing, he [Brian] switched on the studio intercom and said, 'I don't think that sounded quite right, John.' John looked up at him and said in his most cutting voice: 'You stick to your percentages, Brian. We'll look after the music'."

Other areas of Brian's life were in complete disarray. Mersey Beat was now history, and few of the NEMS acts were enjoying

consistent success. Brian's personal life was as turbulent as ever, and almost certainly involved 'silence' payments to sexual extortionists. At the end of 1966, desperately depressed, he took an overdose of pills. Despite psychiatric help, he tried again early in 1967. Even a return to his beloved theatre productions failed to help.

On Thursday August 24, Patti Harrison persuaded The Beatles to go and listen to an Indian guru talk about attaining peace through meditation. They were impressed, and when Maharishi Mahesh Yogi then invited the group to attend that weekend's course at Bangor University in Wales, they leapt at the chance. Brian, who claimed to have plans to meet friends at his country home on Friday, turned down the invitation. He was found dead in his bed on Sunday morning. The cause was an overdose of sleeping pills.

There remains uncertainty over the death. It was registered as accidental, although some have suggested alternatives, among them the idea that it may have been murder, linked to

Above: The Beatles in Bangor, North Wales, having been informed of the death of their former mentor and manager Brian Epstein.

Opposite above: The Beatles take a coach trip to the west country.

Opposite below: Film poster for *Magical Mystery Tour*.

some intrigue relating to Beatles merchandising – support is claimed from the death a year later of David Jacobs, who had signed the merchandising deal, and who had begged for police protection in the weeks leading up to his death.

THE MAGICAL MYSTERY TOUR

Brian's death made The Beatles, if anything, even more resolute about controlling their own affairs. After the triple triumph of 'Strawberry Fields Forever', *Sgt. Pepper* and the rave reception of 'All You Need Is Love' debuted as part of the world's first live global TV broadcast, The Beatles could be forgiven for thinking that they were invincible. The project they had just begun as Brian died was a television musical, *Magical Mystery Tour*. They launched into it like a bunch of first-year film-school students with an unfeasibly large budget, doing everything themselves. It was a shambles.

At the heart of the problem was simply the logistics of organizing such a project – precisely the type of thing at which Brian had always excelled. The filming was a fiasco. Viewing the project as if it were an English working-class seaside outing, Paul populated a tour bus with sideshow freaks and renegades from the musical hall era to travel around with The Beatles and experience the magic of the English countryside. With no itinerary, no permissions and no advance bookings for catering, accommodation or facilities, the whole event took on a surreal absurdity. It took the band 11 weeks to edit their material down to a single hour-long programme.

The soundtrack, a pair of EPs, received reasonable interest, but after the spectacle of *Sgt. Pepper*'s it's no great surprise that the critics weren't wowed. It yield one *bona fide* Beatle classic, though. John's 'I Am The Walrus' featured a fabulous set of nonsense lyrics written, at least in part, to cock a snook at the hordes of critics who insisted on analyzing the band's every word. If the response to the soundtrack was lukewarm, the film itself received outright hostility. With the passing of time *Magical Mystery Tour* has been reappraised more as simply a quirky little Beatles home movie – nothing more.

SGT. PEPPER'S LONELY HEARTS CLUB BAND

Parlophone PCS 7027
Producer: George Martin
Release: June 1, 1967

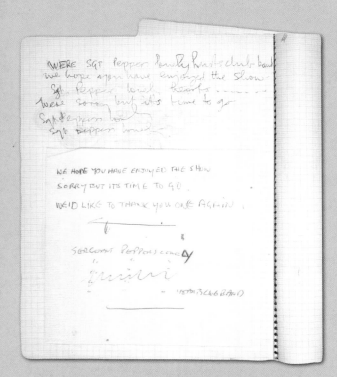

SIDE ONE

SGT. PEPPER'S LONELY HEARTS CLUB BAND
(Lennon/McCartney)

It is as if The Beatles knew that for some, their magnum opus might be considered a little pretentious. The album self-mockingly heralds its own importance with the sounds of an orchestra tuning before it launches into its overture. Paul wrote and sang 'Sgt. Pepper's Lonely Hearts Club Band'. Sound effects from Abbey Road's archives were used to give the impression of a live band. The song ends with an introduction to "the one and only Billy Shears", who sings the next number.

WITH A LITTLE HELP FROM MY FRIENDS
(Lennon/McCartney)

The "Billy Shears" in question is Ringo, giving probably his most effective vocal as a Beatle. The song was written by Paul under a working title of 'Bad Finger Boogie'. There have been over a hundred covers of this song – the most successful being a charity number one hit for Scottish group Wet Wet Wet in 1988. On the reverse of that double "A" sided single, protest singer Billy Bragg could be heard giving an effective rendition of 'She's Leaving Home'. Joe Cocker's radical re-arrangement of the song also hit the number one spot in October 1968.

LUCY IN THE SKY WITH DIAMONDS
(Lennon/McCartney)

The subject of endless speculation, given that the initials of the song are LSD. John always denied any drug reference, claiming that the idea came from a painting by his four-year-old son Julian. When asked what the painting was about, Julian replied, "It's Lucy in the sky with diamonds". Paul sometimes found the endless quest for hidden meaning in their work to be beyond belief: "When you write a song and you mean it one way, and then someone comes up and says something about it that you didn't think of, you can't deny it… people came up and said very cunningly, 'Right, I get it. L–S–D,' but we never thought about it." Interestingly, for what is considered by many to be John Lennon and The Beatles at their best, John was never satisfied with this version, preferring Elton John's 1974 hit single.

GETTING BETTER
(Lennon/McCartney)

It was rare these days for Lennon and McCartney to collaborate as songwriters. This is an exception. The inspiration for the song came from their old stand-in drummer Jimmy Nicol, who could often be heard uttering the phrase.

FIXING A HOLE
(Lennon/McCartney)

Written by Paul, 'Fixing a Hole' is a simple physical/mental analogy. Some have speculated that the song has a drug-related meaning, referring to a heroin fix. Paul was strenuous in his denial: "If you're a junkie sitting in your room fixing a hole, then that's what it will mean to you." As Paul was the Beatle who was always most wary of experimenting with drugs, it would seem highly unlikely that there is any such hidden meaning intended.

Above: Draft lyrics to 'Sgt. Pepper's Lonely Hearts Club Band' in Paul McCartney's notebook.

Opposite: Ringo films a scarf waved by John during recording sessions for the *Sgt. Pepper's Lonely Hearts Club Band* album.

Overleaf: Brian Epstein hosts a dinner party to mark the launch of *Sgt. Pepper's Lonely Hearts Club Band*, May 19 1967.

SHE'S LEAVING HOME

(Lennon/McCartney)

Paul's simple story of a lonely girl who runs away from home to be with her "man from the motor trade" features one of The Beatles most unusual instrumental line-ups. Paul had asked George Martin to score the piece but he had not been available at that time, so Mike Leander stepped in. The Beatles sing but do not play their instruments. Sheila Bromberg plays the harp, accompanied by a nine-piece string ensemble. Paul had taken the inspiration from a story in the *Daily Mirror* newspaper where, "… this girl left home and her father said: 'We gave her everything, I don't know why she left home.'"

BEING FOR THE BENEFIT OF MR. KITE!

(Lennon/McCartney)

John Lennon took little credit for the lyrics for the number that closed the first side: "It was from this poster that I'd bought in an antique shop… advertising a show which starred Mr Kite. It said the Hendersons would also be there, late of Pablois Fanques Fair. There were hoops and horses and someone going through a hogshead of real fire … all at Bishopsgate … I hardly made up a word." As Paul added later, "… you couldn't make that up!"

A number of interesting sound effects were also added. John intended to create a carnival atmosphere, and wanted to use a fairground steam organ. Such an instrument was not available, so George Martin got hold of a recording of a calliope and cut up the tapes, mixed them up, and reassembled them.

SIDE TWO

WITHIN YOU WITHOUT YOU

(Harrison)

It was now expected that George Harrison would provide an Indian interlude to the proceedings. He duly obliged with his overlong spiritual epic 'Within You Without You'. The song was written at Klaus Voorman's house – George discovering a harmonium in one of the rooms. George is the only Beatle to appear on the track. Other instruments are played by members of the Asian Music Circle, although George Martin added a score for a twelve-piece string section.

WHEN I'M SIXTY-FOUR

(Lennon/McCartney)

The first track on the album to be completed, Paul wrote the song at the age of 16, but dusted it down in honour of his father's sixty-fourth birthday.

LOVELY RITA

(Lennon/McCartney)

Paul tells the story: "I was bopping about on the piano … when someone told me that in America they call parking-meter women 'meter maids' … I was thinking vaguely that it should be a hate song: 'You took my car away and I'm so blue today' … but then I thought it would be better to love her."

GOOD MORNING GOOD MORNING

(Lennon/McCartney)

When composing, John would often have the television on at a very low volume in the background. This sometimes inspired his lyrics: "… I heard 'Good Morning, good morning'. It was a cornflakes advertisement." So a song was born.

SGT. PEPPER'S LONELY HEARTS CLUB BAND

(Lennon/McCartney)

A reprise of the opening track. Ending the "theme" of the album (such as it was), it makes way for that most celebrated epilogue:

A DAY IN THE LIFE

(Lennon/McCartney)

For many, this track represents the pinnacle of achievement for The Beatles. It was a genuine collaboration with John writing the opening and ending, and Paul penning the middle section. There had been a 24-bar gap in the song when the three sections were linked. Paul suggested closing the gap with, as John put it, "a sound building up from nothing to the end of the world." Martin hired 40 orchestral musicians, and instructed them to play without a score, as they pleased. The songs ends with a crashing piano chord that takes a full 40 seconds before the reverberation fades out. After that, the listener is greeted by a collage of backwards sounds that lock in the final run-off groove, a last thumbed nose to the analysts.

GEORGE HARRISON

George was born on February 25, 1943. His father Harry had originally been a steward on a passenger ship, but lost his job during the depression. He now worked for Liverpool corporation as a bus conductor. Louise, George's mother, had worked in a greengrocer's shop before starting a family. When compared to John or Paul's Liverpool upbringing, George's early years were a much earthier affair.

George Harrison was the youngest of four children, three boys and a girl. The eldest, his sister Louise, was almost twelve years older than he was, and one of his brothers, Harry, was eight years older. The other brother, Peter, was closer to his age, having been born in July 1940. Even so, George was definitely the baby of the household. His parents were both Liverpool natives. Louise, his mother, came from a partly Irish background – her father, John French, had moved to Liverpool from County Wexford in Ireland. Once in Liverpool, French married a local woman. George's father, Harry Harrison, was a former steward for the White Star Line, and had gone on to work on the buses.

At the time of George's birth, the family lived in very modest conditions in a small home in a terrace in Liverpool's Wavertree district. Number 12 Arnold Grove had an outside lavatory, one coal fireplace as the home's sole source of heating, and it backed on to an alleyway. The Harrisons were finally offered council housing when George was seven, and moved from Wavertree to Speke with what must have been a certain amount of relief.

George's early education took place at the same school as John Lennon – Dovedale Primary. The two had no specific contact however, because George, being much younger, was in a different school year. Indeed, they were largely unaware of one another. Having passed his Eleven-Plus examinations, in 1954 George won a place at the Liverpool Institute, the same grammar school that Paul McCartney attended.

George quickly developed a hatred for all kinds of formal teaching. Unlike Lennon, he didn't cause trouble or make a nuisance of himself. He rebelled quietly, simply refusing to take part in school life. By the age of 13, he had found solace in the guitar and skiffle music. He borrowed the money from his mother to buy a good guitar – one with a cutaway at the top of the body. He paid off the debt by taking a Saturday morning delivery round at his local butcher's shop. Together with his nearest brother, Peter, and a schoolfriend called Arthur Kelly, George formed a skiffle band named The Rebels. This was really the only pursuit that George cared about. With George in The Rebels and Paul McCartney in The Quarrymen, and both the schoolmates being more interested in rock 'n' roll than in school, it's no real surprise that the two boys met and became friends.

Despite being keen to join John and Paul in the Quarrymen, George was initially kept out because of his age. That didn't stop him hanging around the group however, and because he was always available to fill a gap, he did get to play with them from time to time. He gradually became an accepted member of the group, and by the time he reached the age of 16, he was a fully-fledged Quarryman in his own right – albeit one who was still treated as the baby of the group. For all its familiarity from his home life, this role was still rather frustrating. It was one that would haunt him through his entire Beatles career.

Right: A Gibson SG electric guitar belonging to George Harrison was sold by Christie's auction house for $567,50 in 2004.

Opposite: A young George Harrison poses for a portrait playing his first acoustic guitar.

"THE WORLD USED THE BEATLES AS AN EXCUSE TO GO MAD."

George's final thoughts on The Beatles' fame were revealed in *The Beatles Anthology* documentary.

The Liverpool Institute

The Liverpool Mechanics' School of Arts was established in 1825. Like many other similar institutes of the time, it was founded to provide evening education to working men and to offer casual lectures to the general public on topics ranging from evolution to Shakespeare's plays. In 1832, it shortened its name to the Liverpool Mechanics' Institution, and by 1840 it was also offering day school services to boys. It then opened a girl's school across the road in 1844, one of the first public girls' schools in the country. By the early 1850s, the Institution's evening art classes were becoming so important that it was developing an art school in its own right. In 1856 the name changed again to reflect this, to The Liverpool Institute and School of Arts.

Over the next century, the Liverpool Institute developed a strong reputation as an excellent seat of learning, with hundreds of students going on to scholarships at the prestigious Oxford and Cambridge universities. Governors decided to give the school and its assets to the city of Liverpool in 1905, and it became the cornerstones of Liverpool's city education system. It was renamed to the Liverpool Institute High School for Boys, and remained the jewel in Liverpool's academic crown until the fall of selective schooling — the grammar school system — in the late 1960s.

The Liverpool Institute closed in 1985 after twenty years of neglect. Paul McCartney was horrified. George Martin knew that his acquaintance Mark Featherstone-Witty had been inspired by the movie *Fame*, and wanted to set up a British version of the New York High School for the Performing Arts. He put the two in touch, and after seven years of hard wrangling on Featherstone-Witty's part, and a good deal of Paul's money, the building re-opened as the Liverpool Institute for the Performing Arts in 1996. Its graduates include prominent US rocker Liam Lynch, TV presenter Dawn Porter, and Hollyoaks star Leah Hackett.

Schoolwork had been of total disinterest to George for years, and he quietly left at around the same time as he finally cemented his place in the band. He found an apprenticeship as an electrician at one of the Liverpool department stores, Blacklers. This fell by the wayside when The Beatles were offered their first stint in Germany. George continued taking his guitar-playing seriously however, using the long Hamburg sets to hone his skills, and then getting further instruction from Tony Sheridan on top of it. Although George's youth was the start of the band's deportation debacle during that first Hamburg stint, no-one blamed him for any of the subsequent hassle.

George was always considered handsome, and had a great number of devoted female followers. He made the mistake of confessing in an early interview that he had a particular fondness for jelly babies, and from then onwards, fans sent box after box of jelly babies, and sometimes even threw them at the band at live concerts. When Beatlemania crossed the Atlantic, newly devoted American fans picked up on this. However, since jelly babies didn't exist over there, the American fans decided that jelly beans were the same sort of thing. Unfortunately, whilst jelly babies are soft and spongy, American jelly beans are hard-shelled: the band were disturbed to find that their mid-set confectionery showers had started to sting!

Above: George Harrison smokes a cigar and presents a small selection of 21st birthday cards sent to him by Beatles fans.

THE BEGINNING OF THE END

Without Brian, the group were letting their energies fly off in every imaginable direction. They had now been together for years, and things were starting to become stressed. In spite of periodic efforts to regroup, 1968 demonstrated that The Beatles were now basically four individuals intent on doing their own thing.

Having started The Apple Boutique, the band decided to build a business empire. The next stage was Apple Electronics. John Lennon had met a self-proclaimed electronics wizard named Alexis Mardas. "Magic Alex" created all kinds of gizmos that fascinated John. His favourite was the Nothing Box, a small box which displayed red lights at random. He used to watch it for hours on LSD, entranced.

Mardas was given funding to pursue various ideas. He also planned to build a near-miraculous 72-track recording studio to replace Abbey Road, which he declared old-fashioned. George Martin – upgrading the studio from four to eight-track at the time – was not impressed. Further 'Apple' businesses were added – Apple Records, Apple Films, Apple Publishing, all under the umbrella of Apple Corps Ltd, which also represented The Beatles' musical interests collectively.

A PERIOD OF MEDITATION

With a new single, 'Lady Madonna', ready for release, The Beatles headed to India in February to study meditation. Their guru, Maharishi Mahesh Yogi, had an ashram (retreat) overlooking the river Ganges, where he taught students from around the world. Other celebrities joined the band and their wives, including actress Mia Farrow. Instruction time was divided between spiritual teachings, meditation and chanting.

Ringo lasted ten days. He couldn't get on with the food. After two months, Paul and Jane threw in the towel. John and George stayed on, and Alex Mardas flew out to join them. He

was sceptical of the guru. Eventually he revealed to the pair that the guru had made inappropriate sexual advances towards Farrow. Faith shattered, the group let Mardas hustle them away. There is still doubt regarding the truth of Mardas' accusation, Cynthia Lennon suspecting him of jealous manipulation. Paul has said that he didn't believe the accusation, and Farrow's autobiography states that she believes it may have been a misunderstanding.

Despite the controversy, the experience was a positive one. John used it to control his drug dependency, and the austere surroundings had encouraged the band into creative endeavours. In all, they came back from India with more than 30 new songs.

MAHARISHI MAHESH YOGI

The Beatles' spiritual guru was born Mahesh Prasad Varma, in the Panduka area of Raipur, India on January 12, 1917. He graduated in physics before becoming the assistant and disciple of 'Guru Dev', the spiritual leader of a monastery near the Tibetan border. After the Guru died in 1953, Mahesh began coaching students in a meditation technique learnt from his master, which he called Transcendental Meditation. He started teaching internationally in 1958.

In brief, Transcendental Meditation involves sitting for a period, eyes closed, and repeating a specific sound so as to quieten the mind. It does not involve any mental concentration or reflection. Repeated serious scientific and medical studies

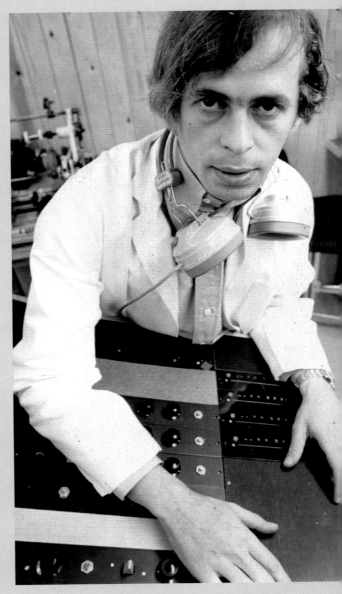

have shown that regular practice can reduce blood pressure, insomnia, nervous exhaustion and anxiety. Some studies have also shown beneficial influence on mental performance.

Over the decades, Mahesh continued teaching and introducing other programs and practices, including a group-practice system called TM-Sidhi, and an initiative to build 'Peace Palace' meditation centres around the world in the hope of "improving humanity's global consciousness". He died on February 5, 2008, and was praised by both Paul and Ringo.

THE ROTTEN APPLE

The Beatles were selling as well as ever, but their business affairs were out of control. Without Brian, they were flailing. The Apple Boutique was the first casualty. On July 29, The Beatles and their families went in and took anything they fancied. The next day, they invited the public to do the same. Afterwards, the doors closed for good.

There was no shortage of would-be managers desperate to take Brian's role and grab a share of the action. With everything in such a mess, John took the initiative and arranged a meeting with Allen Klein, America's foremost showbiz lawyer. He liked the fact that Klein wasn't a "suit" like all the others. George and Ringo were happy to go with it, but Paul was a different matter. He had become 'linked' with New York photographer Linda Eastman in 1967, prompting Jane Asher's departure. Paul's relationship with Linda flourished, and they became engaged. Linda's father and brother were partners in the New York law firm Eastman and Eastman, and Paul wanted them to represent

The Beatles. It was an acrimonious time. Eventually, an uneasy alliance put Klein in charge. It wasn't the unified management that The Beatles needed though, with Paul's interests seeming at odds with the others. Ultimately, it would pull the band apart.

JOHN'S NEW OBSESSION

In May, with Cynthia away on holiday, John invited Japanese avant-garde artist Yoko Ono to work on a series of sound collages. They immediately became virtually inseparable. In the past, only band members had been allowed in the studio during recording sessions, but now Yoko was constantly by John's side. This created bad feeling within the group, as did Paul's increasing domination of Ringo and George. Despite the tensions, the band managed to produce the uplifting 'Hey Jude', a song that Paul wrote for John and Cynthia's son, Julian. It became the biggest-selling single of the year.

From May until October, The Beatles worked solidly in the studio – in fact, often several studios at the same time. Although they band played together on most of the tracks, the songs were invariably finished alone. Only Paul attended studio sessions every single day. The result was the magnificent double-LP *The Beatles*, known universally as *The White Album*.

June 1968 saw the release of *Yellow Submarine*, The Beatles' 'cartoon' film. The band had only minimal involvement in the project, but the film was a triumph of animation and is now viewed as a classic of its type.

Opposite: Magic Alex Mardas, head of Apple Electronics.

Above: *Magical Mystery Tour* party invitation, 1967 and Flyer from Japan tour, 1966.

Overleaf: The Beatles, and friends, travel to India, February 1968.

THE WHITE ALBUM

Label: Parlophone PCS 6067-8
Producer: George Martin
Release: November 22, 1968

SIDE ONE

BACK IN THE USSR
(Lennon/McCartney)

Written by Paul McCartney, 'Back in the USSR' was intended as a 'Soviet' equivalent to Chuck Berry's 'Back in the USA'. Interviewed by *Playboy* magazine in 1984, he said: "I wrote that as a kind of Beach Boys parody… I just liked the idea of Georgia girls and talking about places like the Ukraine as if they were California, you know? It was also 'hands across the water', which I'm still conscious of… they like us out there, even though the bosses in the Kremlin may not. The kids do. And that to me is very important for the future of the race."

The chorus certainly bears this up, featuring precisely the falsetto backing vocals heard on many the Beach Boys songs. Interestingly, both George and John play bass on the track.

DEAR PRUDENCE
(Lennon/McCartney)

Written by John for Prudence Farrow, the younger sister of Mia Farrow. Both sisters were in Rishikesh at the same time as The Beatles. Prudence, against the advice of the Maharishi, would spend unduly long periods in meditation – so much so that she was assigned a full-time nurse. Post-punk band Siouxsie and the Banshees took the song into the Top 10 in 1983.

GLASS ONION
(Lennon/McCartney)

Another of John's digs at those who would ascribe hidden meanings to their songs: "Whatever people make of it afterwards is valid but it doesn't have to correspond with my thoughts … the mystery and shit which is built around all forms of art needs smashing anyway."

The song contains references to a number of previous Beatles tracks, and is written in a way that would seem to be answering questions. For example, he claims that the walrus in 'I Am the Walrus' was Paul.

One of the first bands signed to The Beatles' Apple label was a Welsh group called the Iveys. Needing a change of name, John had wanted to call them Glass Onion – instead they chose Badfinger after Paul's working title for 'A Little Help from My Friends'. They achieved considerable success in the early 1970s.

OB-LA-DI, OB-LA-DA
(Lennon/McCartney)

An early attempt at a white reggae sound. Written by Paul, the song's title comes from a Yoruban phrase by Nigerian percussionist Jimmy Scott, apparently meaning "Life goes on". John was known to have detested 'Ob-La-Di, Ob-La-Da'. Scottish group Marmalade took the song to the top of the charts.

WILD HONEY PIE
(Lennon/McCartney)

A short repetitive chant written and produced entirely by Paul.

THE CONTINUING STORY OF BUNGALOW BILL
(Lennon/McCartney)

Written by John based on a true incident in Rishikesh. A clean-cut American college boy – Richard A. Cooke III – visited his mother who was attending the same course as The Beatles.

The pair went on a hunting expedition and he killed a tiger. John was present when the Maharishi admonished them for their behaviour. According to John: "It was written about a guy in Maharishi's meditation camp who took a short break to go shoot a few poor tigers, and then came back to commune with God. There used to be a character called Jungle Jim, and I combined him with Buffalo Bill. It's sort of a teenage social-comment song and a bit of a joke." Yoko Ono sings one line of the final verse and joins in with the choruses.

WHILE MY GUITAR GENTLY WEEPS
(Harrison)

Written by George and featuring the superb lead guitar work of Eric Clapton. The song was inspired by George's reading of the *I Ching* – the Chinese book of change.

HAPPINESS IS A WARM GUN
(Lennon/McCartney)

The title and chorus were taken directly from the cover of a gun magazine that belonged to George Martin. John spotted the headline and thought it was too good an opportunity to miss. Other phrases used in the song came about as a result of a communal acid trip with Derek Taylor, Pete Shotton and Neil Aspinall.

Opposite: Portraits of The Beatles, included as inserts with *The White Album*.

MARTHA MY DEAR

(Lennon/McCartney)

One of Paul's simple love songs, inspired by Martha, his old English sheep dog. It was also purported to have referred to the ending of his relationship with Jane Asher. Unusually for The Beatles this was not recorded at Abbey Road, but at London's Trident Studios.

I'M SO TIRED

(Lennon/McCartney)

During the time spent with the Maharishi, John found that the amount of time he was spending in meditation meant that he was unable to sleep. He was also missing some of his home comforts – "… curse Sir Walter Raleigh, he was such a stupid get."

BLACKBIRD

(Lennon/McCartney)

Written and recorded by Paul McCartney using an altered tuning on a Martin D28 acoustic guitar. McCartney has said that it was a creative outpouring that saw words and music fall straight into place. The song was written at Paul's farm in Scotland as a response to the unfolding racial tensions taking place in the US during the Spring of 1968. The music was inspired by Bach's 'Bourée in E Minor'.

PIGGIES

(Harrison)

George's 'Piggies' is a gentle mocking of middle class behaviour. However, this was not the interpretation of a struggling Californian musician named Charles Manson. To him, it was no less than a call to arms. Manson and his followers went on to commit a series of murders, the most prominent victim being film star Sharon Tate. At one of the murder scenes the word "pigs" was daubed in the victim's blood.

ROCKY RACCOON

(Lennon/McCartney)

Paul's Western scenario – originally called 'Rocky Sassoon' – was written on a roof-top in Rishikesh with some help from John Lennon and Donovan. George plays bass, John plays harmonium and George Martin plays the bar-room honky-tonk piano.

DON'T PASS ME BY

(Starkey)

Ringo's first sole credit as a composer was written and offered to The Beatles five years earlier. While Ringo shows no signs of lyrical genius, it does contain the memorable couplet: "I'm sorry that I doubted you – I was so unfair/You were in a car crash and you lost your hair."

WHY DON'T WE DO IT IN THE ROAD

(Lennon/McCartney)

Written by Paul, rather in the style of John Lennon. This snippet features Paul playing everything.

I WILL

(Lennon/McCartney)

Paul's simple love song somehow took 67 takes to get right!

JULIA

(Lennon/McCartney)

John Lennon's 'Julia' seems to be written about his mother, killed in a car accident in 1958. But some of the phrases used are clearly inspired by his new love Yoko – for example, her name in Japanese means "child of the ocean". John plays the acoustic guitar – Donovan had taught him finger-picking techniques while at Rishikesh.

SIDE THREE

BIRTHDAY

(Lennon/McCartney)

Paul's rock and roller was written in the studio. Paul has said that 'Birthday' is one of his favourite tracks on the album. John, however, was less impressed: "It's a piece of garbage," was his considered view in 1980.

YER BLUES

(Lennon/McCartney)

John's desperate blues was written at the height of his marital dilemma between Cynthia and Yoko Ono – a situation that he claims made him feel suicidal. On the way back from India, John told Cynthia that he had not been faithful. Within months he and Yoko had become inseparable partners.

"THE MYSTERY WHICH IS BUILT AROUND ALL FORMS OF ART NEEDS SMASHING."

John Lennon

MOTHER NATURE'S SON

(Lennon/McCartney)

The song was written by Paul after a lecture by the Maharishi. Paul recorded it at Abbey Road in the early hours of the morning after the other Beatles had gone home. A brass overdub was added later. Interestingly enough, the same lecture inspired John to write a song called 'Child of Nature'. Although unused at the time, the song resurfaced in 1971 on Lennon's *Imagine* album with new lyrics as 'Jealous Guy'.

EVERYBODY'S GOT SOMETHING TO HIDE EXCEPT ME AND MY MONKEY

(Lennon/McCartney)

To begin with, the song was known as 'Come On, Come On' after the opening lyrics. According to John, "It was about me and Yoko. Everybody seemed to be paranoid except for us two, who were in the glow of love."

SEXY SADIE

(Lennon/McCartney)

John's song of disillusionment with the Maharishi, which had stemmed from rumours of his interest in The Beatles' money and accusations of making sexual advances to women at Rishikesh. The opening lines were originally, "Maharishi, what have you done?" but John was advised to drop the idea on legal grounds.

HELTER SKELTER

(Lennon/McCartney)

For some time, Paul had wanted to produce something raucous and loud. When he read a review of an apparently similar-sounding new single by the Who he was disappointed. When he heard the song – most likely 'I Can See for Miles' – it was nothing like the one he had in mind, so The Beatles went ahead with 'Helter Skelter', the closest they ever got to heavy rock. Charles Manson also found this track inspiring.

LONG LONG LONG

(Harrison)

George sang and played guitar on his song with Paul providing accompaniment on a Hammond organ. What seems to be a simple love song to Patti is in fact about God.

SIDE FOUR

REVOLUTION 1

(Lennon/McCartney)

A heavier version of this song had already appeared on the flip side of the massively successful 'Hey Jude' single. 'Revolution' is a reply to the various revolutionary bodies who saw John as a natural ally. The key lyrics are "Change your head … free your mind instead." Responding to criticism of 'Revolution', John said, "I'll tell you what's wrong with [the world] – people. Tell me one successful revolution."

HONEY PIE

(Lennon/McCartney)

One of Paul's periodic regressions to the kind of old-time music his father used to play. George plays bass and John executes one of his rare guitar solos.

SAVOY TRUFFLE

(Harrison)

The lyrics to George's 'Savoy Truffle' are taken largely from the different kinds of chocolate found in a Mackintosh's Good News chocolate box. The song's inspiration was Eric Clapton who seems to have been giving a prelude to his well-documented future addictions – in this case, it was an obsession for chocolate.

CRY BABY CRY

(Lennon/McCartney)

John's nursery rhyme song was inspired by TV adverts and Donovan's hippie folk songs that he had been played in India.

REVOLUTION 9

(Lennon/McCartney)

In its own way, 'Revolution 9' is one of The Beatles' most significant tracks and influenced a generation of experimental musicians. It is also probably the most universally loathed piece of music of music The Beatles ever released.

'Revolution 9' is a disturbing eight-and-a-quarter-minute sound collage assembled by John and Yoko. The individual components include muffled conversation, a test tape voice repeating the phrase "number nine", John and Yoko screaming, crowd disturbances, Paul playing the piano as well as some of the orchestral overdubs from 'A Day in the Life'.

John tells the story: "'Revolution 9' was an unconscious picture of what I actually think will happen when it happens … like a drawing of revolution. All the thing was made with loops. I had about 30 loops going, fed them into one basic track… chopping it up, making it backwards … I was just using all the bits to make a montage. I really wanted that released."

John wanted it released as a single, but failed to get his way on the issue. In fact, the other three Beatles were even opposed to its appearance on the album.

GOOD NIGHT

(Lennon/McCartney)

John wrote 'Good Night' as a lullaby for his son Julian. In fact, Ringo is the only Beatle who appears on the recording, singing it over a thirty-piece orchestra.

ADDITIONAL NOTES:

• The packaging concept for *The White Album* was created by artist Richard Hamilton. It was his idea that it should be a plain white sleeve. The gatefold package includes a poster with lyrics on one side and a photomontage on the other. There are also four individual portraits of The Beatles taken by photographer John Kelly. The original gatefold sleeve was sealed at the ends and had the openings for the records at the top.

YELLOW SUBMARINE

Label: Parlophone PCS 7070
Producer: George Martin
Release: January 17, 1969

SIDE ONE

YELLOW SUBMARINE
(Lennon/McCartney)
This is the same version of the song found on the *Revolver* album from 1966.

ONLY A NORTHERN SONG
(Harrison)
George Harrison's song was recorded for the *Sgt. Pepper* sessions but failed to make the final cut. The lyrics show his dissatisfaction with The Beatles' music publishing business. Northern Songs had been set up in 1963 primarily to exploit Lennon/McCartney compositions. The company had been floated in 1965, but whereas Lennon and McCartney each owned 15 per cent of the public company's shares, Harrison owned just 0.8 per cent, so John and Paul, as bigger shareholders, earned more from George's songs than he did himself. As the lyric declares: "It doesn't really matter what chords I play … what words I say … it's only a Northern Song."

ALL TOGETHER NOW
(Lennon/McCartney)
Another of The Beatles' children's songs.

Left: Set of four button badges created to promote the *Yellow Submarine* movie.

Opposite and above: Extracts from *Yellow Submarine*, The Beatles' acclaimed animated movie.

HEY BULLDOG
(Lennon/McCartney)

Written by John, this is one of the rare Beatles songs to be based around a piano riff. Originally intended to be 'Hey Bullfrog', when Paul began barking unexpectedly during the recording they decided to retitle the song. Paul remembered 'Hey Bulldog' with fondness when interviewed in 1994: "I helped him [John] finish it off in the studio, but it's mainly his vibe. There's a little rap at the end between John and I, we went into a crazy little thing at the end. We always tried to make every song different because we figured, 'Why write something like the last one? We've done that.'"

IT'S ALL TOO MUCH
(Harrison)

Another of George's songs recorded for during the *Sgt. Pepper* sessions that failed to make the final cut. It was also slated for possible use in *Magical Mystery Tour*.

ALL YOU NEED IS LOVE
(Lennon/McCartney)

Written to be performed on the first global satellite link, The Beatles were commissioned by the BBC to come up with a simple message that could be understood by all nationalities. It was performed live in London, broadcast to 26 countries and watched by a global audience estimated to be over 400 million.

SIDE TWO

The second side of *Yellow Submarine* contains some of the incidental orchestral music by George Martin, featured throughout the film.

"GEORGE'S HOUSE SEEMED TO BE LIKE A BIG SUBMARINE, AND I WAS DRIVING IT."

John Lennon, on his first LSD trip

RINGO STARR

Richard Starkey (senior) and Elsie Gleave met while working for a baker in Liverpool. By the time they were married in 1936 Richard had begun working on the docks. They lived in a large terraced house in the Dingle, a poor, working-class area. Ringo Starr was born as Richard Starkey Jr on July 7, 1940. His parents' marriage lasted just seven years, with Richard leaving Elsie with little Ritchie in 1943. She moved to a smaller house in the same area, and took work as a barmaid.

Ritchie's education seemed to be doomed from the start. He first attended St. Silas Infant School at the age of five. His schooling was interrupted a year later, when a burst appendix led to peritonitis and a coma. He wasn't expected to survive. Ritchie regained consciousness after ten weeks, and began a slow recovery. One of the presents he was given to keep himself entertained was a drum, which greatly captured his imagination. Six months later, still in hospital, he knocked himself unconscious when he fell out of bed, setting his recovery back further. By the time he finally came home from hospital, Ritchie had been in there for more than a year.

Having lost so much time, Ritchie had fallen badly behind in his schooling, and was placed in a class with much younger children. One of his neighbour's children, a girl named Marie Maguire, taught him how to read and write so that he could start to catch up. Even with her help, though, Ritchie had little interest in school, and soon started to skip classes. These youthful excursions led to an unusually early alcohol problem, suffering blackouts by the age of nine. His schooling never fully recovered – so poor was his work that he wasn't even given the opportunity to sit for the Eleven-Plus examinations.

Ritchie was enthusiastic about Elsie's marriage to house-painter Harry Graves in 1953, who won him over by being so supportive about his musical interests. He and Graves became close, and Ritchie used to jokingly refer to the man as his "step-ladder". After a couple of abortive attempts at finding work, Ritchie became an apprentice joiner at an engineering firm. Along with Eddie Miles, a fellow apprentice, he started a skiffle group. They along with some other colleagues used to entertain the rest of the staff at lunchtimes – Ritchie naturally handling percussion.

For Christmas 1957, Harry Graves bought Ritchie a drum kit in London, lugging it all the way back up to Liverpool on the train. It was a ramshackle second-hand affair, but from that point on it was inevitable that the quiet lad who'd turned to drumming for solace so often in the past would try to make a living as a professional drummer.

Ritchie spent some time playing with the Darktown Skiffle group, and often sat in with other bands, including, in March 1959, a group called Al Caldwell's Texans. Six months later, Ritchie joined the Texans officially. By this time they were calling themselves Rory Storm and the Hurricane. The band dressed outrageously, put on a boisterous stage show, and quickly established themselves as one of Liverpool's top bands. When they were offered a three-month summer booking to play at the Butlins holiday camp in Pwllheli in Wales, Ritchie

Opposite: Ringo at home with mother, Elsie, and step-father, Harry.

Left: Richard Starkey poses with a splendid pompadour haircut.

A Quiet Time

The same year as Elsie married Harry, Ritchie caught a cold which turned into pleurisy (an infection of the lining surrounding the lungs), and then tuberculosis. This led to a further two years in a sanatorium, a specialist hospital designed for lengthy recoveries.

As Starr says: "In those days, they used to put you in what we liked to call a greenhouse in the country – the countryside. And thank God someone had invented Streptomycin. And you just sat around for a year getting well ... So to keep you entertained, once a week, they'd have like lessons: could be knitting, could be modelling, occasionally it was music. And they'd bring in tambourines, triangles and little drums ... [drums] became the dream that one day I would have my own set, which happened. And then the other dream was that I would play with other musicians, which came true."

In spite of all his troubles, Ritchie managed to retain his easy-going, good-natured attitude, although his comparative isolation had left him quiet and thoughtful. When he finally got back home at the age of 15, he saw no point in trying to go back to school. He first found work as a messenger for British Rail, until a standard medical assessment forced him to resign as unfit for what was mainly physical duty. He also worked for a time as a barman on a ferry travelling between Liverpool and Wales, but was eventually fired for being rude to his boss when he turned up drunk one day.

finally had to choose between his apprenticeship – and his fiancée at the time, a girl called Geraldine – and the lure of rock 'n' roll – not to mention an impressive £20 per week. Despite everything his parents, employers and girlfriend could say, music won over.

Vocalist Rory Storm had officially changed his name from Alan Caldwell by deed-poll. He suggested to Ritchie that he should get a stage name for himself. Ritchie was already well-known in the group for wearing rings on every finger, and it wasn't long before Ritchie became Rings, and then Ringo. Starkey was then shortened to Starr so that his solo spots could be called 'Starr Time'. Like Rory, Ringo adopted his new name legally.

Rory Storm and the Hurricanes made the lead billing at the Hamburg Kaiserkeller in November 1960, where Ringo first met The Beatles. In 1961, Rory's group completed a tour of American air bases in France, another summer at Butlins, and then a series of local rounds in Liverpool. Ringo began to tire of the band's stagnation, and even thought seriously about immigrating to America to work in a factory in Texas. Instead he went back to Hamburg again in 1962, playing for Tony Sheridan, before rejoining Rory Storm for yet another Butlins summer season. He was already considering an offer from King Size Taylor and the Dominos when The Beatles made contact in August 1962. He would soon become the most famous drummer in the world.

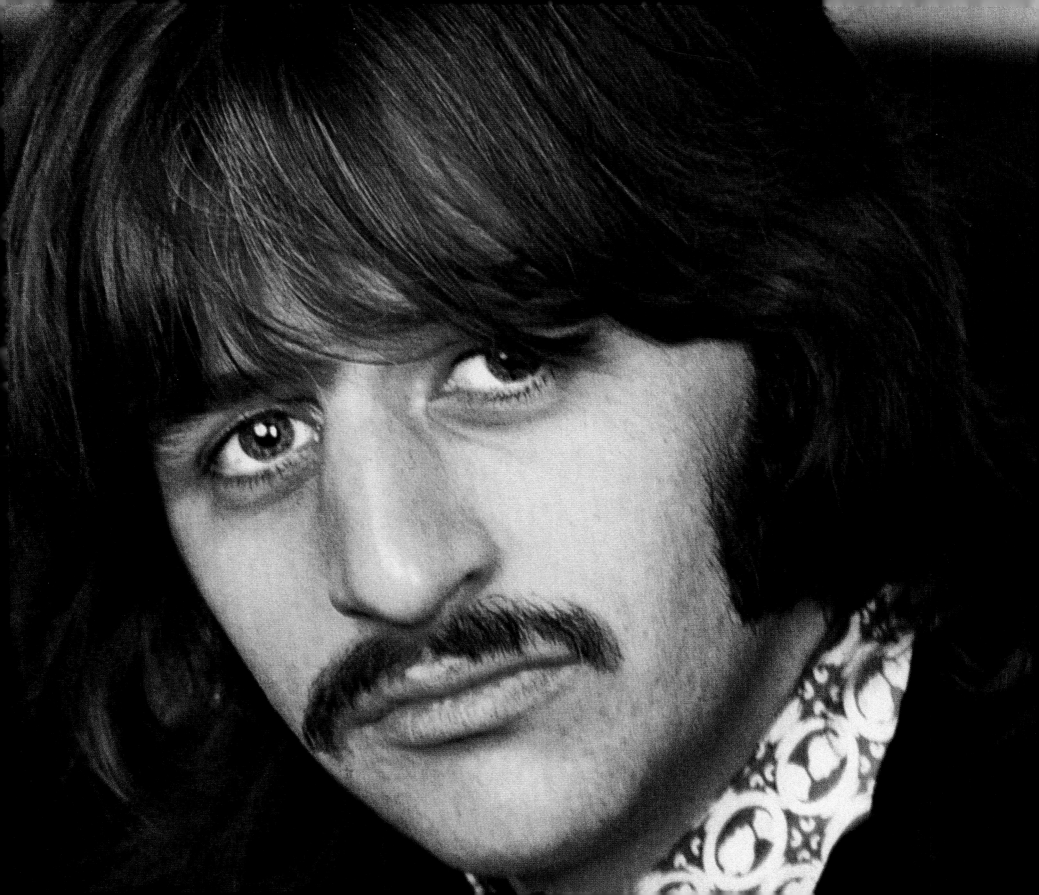

Paul McCartney was now the motivating force behind the band. He saw himself as a born musician with a strong need to perform in front of an audience. His colleagues didn't quite feel the same way. Concerned that apathy was spreading throughout the band, Paul thought a one-off filmed concert might bring some enthusiasm back. The others reluctantly agreed. TV producer Denis O'Dell, hired to organise the event, suggested that rehearsals for the show should be recorded for an alternative television documentary.

When taped rehearsals began at Twickenham Film Studios on January 15, tensions were palpable from the outset. Paul was the only Beatle who really wanted to be there. The other three, for their part, were clearly tired of Paul's over-assertiveness. Shortly after a terse exchange with Paul, George quietly walked out and spent the best part of the next week in Liverpool with his parents. Filming and rehearsals went on without him. He eventually returned with as little overt ado as his departure, following several lengthy negotiation sessions.

Recording for the new album was scheduled to take place in Alex Mardas' new Apple Studios in the basement of Savile Row. At the end of January, The Beatles turned up to start recording, only to find complete chaos and a clearly amateurish attempt at cobbling Frankenstein-like pieces of equipment together. Alex might have possessed a good imagination, but he was incapable of producing anything usable. The next two days were spent undoing Alex's handiwork and hiring mixing consoles from Abbey Road.

The recording went more smoothly than one would have imagined from the rehearsals. As the idea was to return to a more spontaneous, live type of recording, The Beatles brought in an extra musician

– George's friend Billy Preston, an outstanding keyboard player. The presence of an outsider seemed to relax the tensions that had made the Twickenham experience so unbearable. As Paul McCartney said, "You know what it's like when you have company... you try and be on your best behaviour."

UP ON THE ROOF

Meanwhile, plans were being changed behind the scenes. *The White Album* had used up the back-catalogue of new material, and the new songs were taking their time to develop. The budget for filming the live performance couldn't possibly stretch through the recording of an entire album, so an alternative concert idea had to materialise very soon. It was decided that on Thursday, January 30, The Beatles would perform an unannounced concert on the roof of their Savile Row headquarters. This would be the filmed live performance.

At lunchtime on the great day, The Beatles took to the impromptu stage at the top of the building, surrounded by family, friends and film crews, and struck up the opening chords of 'Get Back'. Within minutes local office workers began to investigate the noise. Gradually, Mayfair became more and more congested until the police arrived. Finally, after 42 minutes of playing, the show came to an end with another version of 'Get Back'. That was to be The Beatles' final public performance.

After spending much of February trying to finish the album, their enthusiasm – even Paul's – began to dwindle. The Beatles brought in producer Glyn Johns, handed over the pile of master tapes, and asked him to finish it. None of them even bothered going in. The results were even worse than they had expected. They shelved it, releasing only a pair of singles. Paul's 'Get Back' was released in April, followed by John's 'The Ballad of John and Yoko', on which

NEIL ASPINALL

NEMS ENTERPRISES LTD · 24 Moorfields · Liverpool.2 · CENtral 0793

BEETHOVEN
PLEASE PLEASE ME
SAW HER STANDING
FROM ME TO YOU
TASTE OF HONEY
BOYS
SHE LOVES YOU
TWIST AND SHOUT.

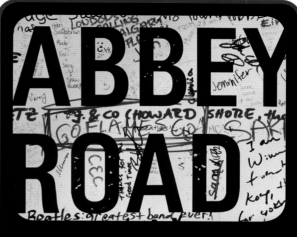

Abbey Road

The sleeve of *Abbey Road*, again eschewing the flashy design conventions of the period, was simplicity itself – a photograph of the four Beatles on a zebra crossing, outside Abbey Road studios. The reverse side shows a close-up of the Abbey Road street sign. Strangely, Paul's bare-footed presence was taken as proof of his demise at the time of a well-documented "Paul is dead" rumour that had begun in America.

The sleeve made Abbey Road the most famous recording studio in the world. Even today, tourists from all over the world continue to make a daily pilgrimage to what would otherwise be an unremarkable street in a suburb of north London. New road signs continue to disappear almost the moment they are put up. The graffiti on the walls outside the studio's car park are a reminder that, 45 years on, fascination with The Beatles remains as strong as ever.

John plays guitars and Paul drums and piano. Both singles were, again, worldwide number one hits.

ONE LAST TRY

The following months saw The Beatles embroiled in legal wrangling of the Klein-Eastman variety. They also started to get more and involved in working on their own projects. For John, Paul and George, these were various shades of music. Ringo on the other hand took the time to star in a darkly satirical movie called *The Magic Christian*, a rather heavy-handed attack on greed and capitalist excess.

Then, in June 1969, Paul McCartney contacted George Martin with an unexpected request. He told George

that The Beatles wanted to record another album with him. Martin agreed to one more try, and Abbey Road was block-booked for the first three weeks of July. Once again, everyone put their differences behind them and concentrated on the one thing that had created such close friendships – music.

The album was to be called, aptly, *Abbey Road*. From its release date at the end of September, it was taken as proof that The Beatles were genuinely 'together' again. While *The White Album* had broken records, *Abbey Road* sold in even greater quantities. It went to number one in the UK, not budging for the next five months. It is now among the biggest selling albums of all time.

If *Abbey Road* was to give their public hope for things to come, The Beatles – John in particular, always knew that it would be their last album. It was a pretty special way to go out. It ends with the vignette 'The End' in which Paul sings, "And in the end the love you take is equal to the love you make." And with that The Beatles and the 1960s – the decade they had all but created – came to an end.

Above: Swamped by fans, Paul McCartney marries Linda Eastman at Marylebone registry office, London.

Opposite: Set list written on the back of Neil Aspinall's business card (later CEO of Apple Corps), Eskilstuna, Sweden.

ABBEY ROAD

Label: Parlophone PCS 7088
Producer: George Martin
Release: September 26, 1969

SIDE ONE

COME TOGETHER
(Lennon/McCartney)
John's composition was written originally as a campaign song for Dr Timothy Leary, who was planning to run for Governor in California. Leary's campaign had barely begun when he was convicted of possessing marijuana.

SOMETHING
(Harrison)
George Harrison wrote this song – dedicated to his wife Patti (who eventually left him for his best friend Eric Clapton) – for inclusion on the *The White Album*. Released as a single, although it fared badly by Beatle standards by only just scraping into the Top 5, it has become something of standard, being the second most covered Beatles song after 'Yesterday'.

MAXWELL'S SILVER HAMMER
(Lennon/McCartney)
According to Paul: "[The song] epitomizes the downfalls of life. Just when everything is going smoothly 'bang bang' down comes Maxwell's silver hammer and ruins everything." For John, 'Maxwell's Silver Hammer' was Paul at his worst.

OH DARLING
(Lennon/McCartney)
Inspired by the doo-wop singers of the 1950s, Paul "… came into the studios early every day for a week to sing it by myself … I wanted to sound as though I'd been performing all week." In spite of Paul's efforts, John always thought he could've done a better job.

OCTOPUS'S GARDEN
(Starkey)
During a boating holiday in Sardinia, Ringo was told by the ship's captain about the way octopuses lived. This apparently inspired Ringo to write his second song for The Beatles. George felt that Ringo was composing "cosmic songs without noticing it."

I WANT YOU
(SHE'S SO HEAVY)

(Lennon/McCartney)
One of the simplest love songs ever written. John says: "This is about Yoko … there was nothing else I could say about her other than I want you, she's so heavy." Annoyed when criticized for being trite, Lennon argued, "When you're drowning you don't say 'I would be incredibly pleased if someone would have the foresight to notice me drowning and come and help me', you just scream."

SIDE TWO

HERE COMES THE SUN
(Harrison)
Written on a sunny afternoon in Eric Clapton's garden, George felt relief at having escaped from a tense business meeting with Allen Klein. 'Here Comes the Sun' is another of George's best-known compositions – it features the first Beatles use of a Moog synthesiser. In 1976 Steve Harley and Cockney Rebel took their own version of the song into the British hit parade.

BECAUSE
(Lennon/McCartney)
John's 'Because' decribes the early days of his relationship with Yoko. The song's chord structure was inspired by Beethoven's 'Moonlight Sonata', which Yoko Ono would often play on John's grand piano.

YOU NEVER GIVE ME YOUR MONEY
(Lennon/McCartney)
A song written by Paul in three parts. This is the first of a medley of short or half-finished songs which are segued and take up much of side two of the album.

SUN KING
(Lennon/McCartney)
The song starts with a guitar instrumental clearly inspired by Fleetwood Mac's 'Albatross', which had been a major worldwide hit six months earlier. John originally called the track 'Los Paranoias', most probably because of the random Italian, Spanish and Portuguese words that make up the last verse. It has also been suggested that Lennon was parodying Paul McCartney's French verse in the middle of 'Michelle', recorded four years earlier.

MEAN MR MUSTARD
(Lennon/McCartney)
John wrote this vignette in India, inspired by a newspaper story of a man who habitually hid his money away. John originally wrote about his sister Shirley, but changed the name to Pam for the track that followed.

POLYTHENE PAM

(Lennon/McCartney)

At the time of the album's release, John claimed to have sung 'Polythene Pam' in a thick Liverpool accent: "…because it was supposed to be about a mythical Liverpool scrubber dressed up in her jackboots and kilt." He later admitted that it was a composite of a character from their Cavern days, known as Polythene Pat, and a girl he had met in 1963 with the British beat poet Royston Ellis.

SHE CAME IN THROUGH THE BATHROOM WINDOW

(Lennon/McCartney)

Written by Paul after his St John's Wood house had been broken into by one of the many fans who would routinely loiter outside. These hangers-on would later become immortalized as 'Apple Scruffs' on George's *All Things Must Pass* album.

GOLDEN SLUMBERS

(Lennon/McCartney)

According to Paul: "I came across the traditional tune 'Golden Slumbers' in a song book of Ruth's [his stepsister]. And I thought it would be nice to write my own."

CARRY THAT WEIGHT

(Lennon/McCartney)

Sharply edited into the back of the previous track, 'Carry That Weight' was written by Paul, with vocals by all four Beatles.

THE END

(Lennon/McCartney)

The number opens with Ringo's only ever drum solo, followed by three guitar solos – one each from John, Paul and George.

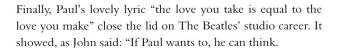

Finally, Paul's lovely lyric "the love you take is equal to the love you make" close the lid on The Beatles' studio career. It showed, as John said: "If Paul wants to, he can think.

ADDITIONAL NOTES:

• After a gap of 20 seconds, Paul's throwaway 23-second ragtime 'Her Majesty' appears. The song is not listed on the cover of the original issue of the album, although it does appear on the record label.

"IF PAUL WANTS TO, HE CAN THINK."

John Lennon, on his songwriting partner.

LET IT BE

Label: Parlophone PCS 7096
Producer: George Martin, Phil Spector, Glyn Johns
Release: May 8, 1970

SIDE ONE

TWO OF US
(Lennon/McCartney)

Paul's 'Two of Us' is a love song to the new woman in his life, Linda Eastman. It is introduced on the album by John Lennon as: "'I Dig a Pygmy' by Charles Hawtry and the Deaf Aids." Charles Hawtry was a legendary English comedy actor, who featured in the famous *Carry On …* series of films. The Deaf Aids was a nickname given by The Beatles to their Vox amplifiers.

The song was first recorded by New York group Mortimer, who had been signed to The Beatles' Apple label, but it was never issued.

DIG A PONY
(Lennon/McCartney)

A song that perhaps indicates the Beatle state of mind during the Get Back sessions. A composite of two different songs written by John, and put together in the studio, 'Dig a Pony' makes little sense at all. In an interview a few months before his death, he declared that it was: "…just another piece of garbage."

ACROSS THE UNIVERSE
(Lennon/McCartney)

A version of 'Across the Universe' had already been released in 1968 on a World Wildlife Fund benefit album. John had not cared for that take, and wanted to make a new recording. The *Let It Be* version features John singing solo with an acoustic guitar, backed by an orchestra and choir. The song highlights the impact of the time the band spent in India, including the mantra "Jai guru deva om", a Sanskrit phrase that can translate loosely as "Hail to the divine guru".

I ME MINE
(Harrison)

According to George, the composer: "It's [a song] about the ego … the eternal problem …" The verses are played in waltz time – apparently inspired by a marching band he saw on television. In the *Let It Be* film, John and Yoko can be seen to be dancing to George's performance of the song.

DIG IT
(Lennon/McCartney/Starkey/Harrison)

Edited down from a five-minute jam, John sings about the CIA, the FBI, blues guitarist BB King, and legendary Manchester United football manager Sir Matt Busby.

LET IT BE
(Lennon/McCartney)

Paul's hymn-like 'Let It Be' seems to have been a response to the heavy pressure of the additional responsibilities he took on as unofficial leader after Brian Epstein's death. As he said, "I wrote it when all those business problems started to get me down … writing the song was my way of exorcising ghosts." The original version, with John on bass and Billy Preston on organ, had already been a million-selling hit single two months earlier. An alternative version, in which George plays a different guitar passage, is included on the album.

MAGGIE MAY
(traditional)

John and Paul give a brief rambling rendition of a traditional Liverpool folk song.

SIDE TWO

I'VE GOT A FEELING

(Lennon/McCartney)

Another composite of two songs, this time Paul's 'I've Got a Feeling' and John's 'Everybody Had a Hard Year'. Both composers sing their respective songs, concluding with both parts sung at the same time.

ONE AFTER 909

(Lennon/McCartney)

John and Paul wrote 'One After 909' together in 1959. They first recorded the song in 1963 during the session that produced 'From Me to You'.

THE LONG AND WINDING ROAD

(Lennon/McCartney)

The song that finally caused Paul to snap. He hated Phil Spector's over-the-top additions, and felt that they spoiled the documentary nature of the *Get Back* project. Allen Klein's refusal to restore the original versions was the catalyst for Paul's public resignation. 'The Long and Winding Road' was issued as a single in the US at the same time as the album came out. Needless to say, in spite of Paul's views, it went to number one, selling 1.2 million copies within two days. Paul would have to wait until 2003 for the release of *Let It Be … Naked*, his own no-frills mix of the album, to let the world hear how he had wanted the album to sound.

FOR YOU BLUE

(Harrison)

'George's Blues', as it was first known, follows a traditional 12-bar structure. Perhaps the most unusual thing about it is that while all The Beatles were most definitely feeling the blues, George's are, as he says, "happy-go-lucky!"

GET BACK

(Lennon/McCartney)

Already a worldwide hit over a year earlier, the album presents a different take, ending with John's words, edited from the ending of the rooftop concert.

ADDITIONAL NOTES:

• *Let It Be* was originally only released in a boxed set. It came complete with a book of photographs and dialogue from the film. Six months later, this version was deleted to be replaced by a standard sleeve with no inserts.
• The *Let It Be* album was covered in its entirety in 1988 by Laibach, a political/avant-garde band from Slovenia.

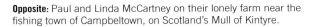

Opposite: Paul and Linda McCartney on their lonely farm near the fishing town of Campbeltown, on Scotland's Mull of Kintyre.

Right: John and Yoko hold a press conference at the Palace Hotel, New York.

Below: George Harrison in discussion with Indian musician Ravi Shankar at London's Royal Festival Hall.

Bottom Right: Ringo and Maureen at London's Heathrow Airport.

1970 ... AND BEYOND

As far as three of The Beatles were concerned, that was pretty much that. Paul still wanted to keep things going, though. On one occasion when Paul again tried to push them into playing live, John told the band that he'd had enough. He wanted out. But this was no revelation – after all, Ringo and George had walked out before, but they always came back. They left things to simmer.

Allen Klein's emergence on the scene had been a dramatic one. He arrived to find Apple Corps in a worse state than he could have imagined. Within months he had pared the organization down to the barest of essentials. Klein had also found The Beatles' contractual affairs in a muddle. The Beatles had mistakenly thought that *Yellow Submarine* constituted the third and final film of their contract with United Artists. They were wrong. Instead of issuing the *Get Back* project as a TV show, Klein turned it into a feature length film that could be sold to United Artists.

Klein's next move was to renegotiate their record deals. This was a problem because John was now insistent that he was leaving the band. Klein asked him to keep silent until he had completed his negotiations. John agreed, although speculation began to increase again in the music press.

The Beatles continued to have little to do with the *Get Back* project – now retitled *Let It Be* after one of Paul's songs on the album. One thing was decided, though – no matter how little they cared about it, the album in its current state was simply not up to scratch. With The Beatles' consent, Klein handed it over to legendary American producer Phil Spector. The finished version of *Let It Be* is in many ways The Beatles' strangest album. Some of the tracks Spector left in a raw and unfinished state, even leaving snippets of dialogue – mostly John's sarcastic quips. The rest of the album was very heavily doctored with the addition of orchestras and brass sections.

Even The Beatles received a surprise. Paul in fact was so furious that he insisted his songs be reverted back to their pre-Spector state. Klein didn't respond, and Paul handed his notice in. That was that.

THE AFTERMATH

By the time of Paul's official announcement on April 10, 1970, few were completely surprised. All four of The Beatles had already started solo careers. It was inevitable that a band that had been so successful – it's members universally known and loved – would spawn solo careers. It was readily assumed that, as two giants of popular music, both Lennon and McCartney would go on to great things.

Paul has lived up to that promise. There isn't the space to do his career justice here, but he is rightly recognized as the most successful composer and musician in the history of popular music. He has been ceaselessly active over the years. Whilst his music may not have always enjoyed the acclaim of his former band, he did emulate some of their commercial success. In the 1970s, with his band Wings, McCartney was one of the biggest selling artists of the decade, with albums such as *Band on the Run*, and multi-million-selling hits like 'Mull of Kintyre'. He also turned his attention to other public projects, campaigning on behalf animal rights, peace groups and other charities. He received a knighthood from the Queen in 1997, and continues to enjoy a hugely successful recording and concert career

including, most recently, closing the 2012 London Olympic's opening ceremony with, 'Hey Jude'.

George Harrison also enjoyed a successful musical career. His first solo album, *All Things Must Pass*, was hugely successful – more so than any other solo Beatle efforts of the time. But his success and output had tailed off by the end of the 1970s. His career was resurrected in 1988 with the Traveling Wilburys – a supergroup made up of George Harrison, Tom Petty, Bob Dylan, Roy Orbison and Jeff Lynne. He also had a prestigious career in both music and film production. George lived a quiet life and rarely made the news, until he was stabbed by

a deranged stalker in December, 1999. Less than two years later, on November 29, 2001, George died after a battle with cancer. Paul often pays tribute to his friend at his concerts by performing a ukulele version of 'Something'.

Ringo enjoyed a string of hit singles and albums in the first half of the 1970s, and has continued to operate at his own pace, often performing with his All Starr band. Ringo has also featured in almost a dozen (non-Beatles) movies, and provided the voice for the first two series of the much-loved children's animation *Thomas the Tank-Engine*.

Of course, John Lennon's post-Beatles story is legendary. Before the band had even split, he and Yoko had become active peace propagandists. Recording together as the Plastic Ono Band, they turned a hostile eye on the establishment. Their first single, 'Give Peace a Chance', was a huge hit despite being performed during a ten-day 'bed-in' in Montreal, Canada, and has since become *the* definitive peace anthem.

In 1971, Lennon hired Phil Spector to produce what has become his signature album, *Imagine*. The title track is probably one of the best-loved pop songs of all time. After the fun and games of the past few years, the new album was produced with accessibility in mind, and featured gentle sounds and coherent lyrics. In September of that year, having had enough of the British press mocking Yoko, the couple moved to New York. John would never again return to the UK.

He had a turbulent time later in the 1970s, in particular with regard to his relationship with Yoko. His musical output throughout that period – albums such as *Mind Games* and *Walls and Bridges* – all sold in healthy quantities but largely failed to live up to the high expectations of critics and fans. By the end of the decade, his marital issues finally sorted, he was devoting himself to living peacefully in New York with Yoko and their son Sean. This triggered a new creative burst, and an album, *Double Fantasy*, emerged on November 17, 1980. Although

no work of genius, it seemed to indicate that one of the great creative minds in popular music was back, ready to tackle a new decade. Sadly, John was dead just three weeks later, shot by an obsessive fan while entering the courtyard of his home. Any lingering public hopes of a Beatles reconciliation were finally laid to rest with him. Lennon's murderer, Mark Chapman, remains imprisoned at the Attica Correctional Facility, Buffalo, New York.

Opposite: Ringo Starr and his All Starr Band perform in support of Ringo's new album *Liverpool 8*, July 23, 2008.

Top Left: Wings perform on TV (L–R: Denny Laine, Linda McCartney, Henry McCullough and Paul McCartney).

Top Right: Group shot of the Traveling Wilburys (L–R: Bob Dylan, Jeff Lynne, Tom Petty, Roy Orbison and George Harrison).

Above Right: John Lennon and Yoko Ono give away their hair, as part of auction for world peace, to Black Power leader Michael X.

DISCOGRAPHY

ORIGINAL UK ALBUMS

22-03-63	*Please Please Me*
22-11-63	*With The Beatles*
10-06-64	*A Hard Day's Night*
04-12-64	*Beatles For Sale*
06-08-65	*Help!*
03-12-65	*Rubber Soul*
05-08-66	*Revolver*
01-06-67	*Sgt. Pepper's Lonely Hearts Club Band*
22-11-68	*The Beatles (The White Album)*
17-01-69	*Yellow Submarine*
26-09-69	*Abbey Road*
08-05-70	*Let It Be*

Official UK Compilation Albums

09-12-66	*A Collection of Beatles Oldies*
19-04-73	*1962–1966 (the Red Album)*
19-04-73	*1967–1970 (the Blue Album)*
19-11-76	*Magical Mystery Tour*
07-03-88	*Past Masters, Volume One*
07-03-88	*Past Masters, Volume Two*
15-11-88	*The Beatles Box Set*
30-11-94	*Live at the BBC*
21-11-95	*Anthology 1*
18-03-96	*Anthology 2*
28-10-96	*Anthology 3*
13-09-99	*Yellow Submarine* Soundtrack
13-11-00	*The Beatles 1*
17-11-03	*Let It Be … Naked*
16-11-04	*The Capitol Albums, Volume 1*
11-04-06	*The Capitol Albums, Volume 2*
20-11-06	*Love*

Original UK Singles

05-10-62	'Love Me Do' / 'P.S. I Love You'
11-01-63	'Please Please Me' / 'Ask Me Why'

11-04-63	'From Me To You' / 'Thank You Girl'
23-08-63	'She Love You' / 'I'll Get You'
29-11-63	'I Want to Hold Your Hand' / This Boy
20-03-64	'Can't Buy me Love' / 'You Can't Do That'
10-07-64	'A Hard Day's Night' / 'Things We Said Today'
27-11-64	'I Feel Fine' / 'She's a Woman'
09-04-65	'Ticket to Ride' / 'Yes It Is'
23-07-65	'Help!' / 'I'm Down'
03-12-65	'We Can Work It Out' / 'Day Tripper'
10-06-66	'Paperback Writer' / 'Rain'
05-08-66	'Yellow Submarine' / 'Eleanor Rigby'
17-02-67	'Strawberry Fields Forever' / 'Penny Lane'
07-07-67	'All You Need Is Love' / 'Baby You're a Rich Man'
24-11-67	'Hello Goodbye' / 'I Am the Walrus'
15-03-68	'Lady Madonna' / 'The Inner Light'
30-08-68	'Hey Jude' / Revolution'
11-04-69	'Get Back' / 'Don't Let Me Down'
30-05-69	'The Ballad of John and Yoko' / 'Old Brown Shoe'
31-10-69	'Something' / 'Come Together'
06-03-70	'Let It Be' / 'You Know My Name'
20-03-95	'Baby It's You' / 'I'll Follow the Sun'
	'Devil in Her Heart' / 'Boys'
12-12-95	'Free as a Bird '/ 'I Saw Her Standing There'
	'This Boy'/ 'Christmas Time'
04-03-96	'Real Love' / 'Baby's in Black'
	'Yellow Submarine' /
	'Here, There and Everywhere'

ORIGINAL UK EPS

12-07-63	*Twist and Shout*
06-09-63	*The Beatles' Hits*
01-11-63	*The Beatles (No. 1)*
07-02-64	*All My Loving*
19-06-64	*Long Tall Sally*
04-11-64	*Extracts from the Film A Hard Day's Night*

06-11-64	*Extracts from the Album A Hard Day's Night*
06-04-65	*Beatles for Sale*
04-06-65	*Beatles for Sale (No. 2)*
06-12-65	*The Beatles' Million Sellers*
04-03-66	*Yesterday*
08-07-66	*Nowhere Man*
08-12-67	*Magical Mystery Tour*

ORIGINAL US ALBUMS

10-01-64	*Introducing … The Beatles*
20-01-64	*Meet The Beatles!*
10-04-64	*The Beatles' Second Album (US album)*
26-06-64	*A Hard Day's Night*
20-07-64	*Something New*
15-12-64	*Beatles '65*
22-03-65	*The Early Beatles*
14-06-65	*Beatles VI*
13-08-65	*Help!*
06-12-65	*Rubber Soul*
16-07-66	*Yesterday … and Today*
08-08-66	*Revolver*
02-06-67	*Sgt. Pepper's Lonely Hearts Club Band*
27-11-67	*Magical Mystery Tour*
25-11-68	*The Beatles (The White Album)*
13-01-69	*Yellow Submarine*
01-10-69	*Abbey Road*
26-02-70	*Hey Jude*
18-05-70	*Let It Be*

ORIGINAL US SINGLES

23-04-62	'My Bonnie' / 'The Saints'
25-02-63	'Please Please Me' / 'From Me to You'
27-05-63	'From Me To You' / 'Thank You Girl'
16-09-63	'She Loves You' / 'I'll Get You'
26-12-63	'I Want To Hold Your Hand' / 'I Saw Her Standing There'
27-01-64	'My Bonnie' / 'The Saints'
30-01-64	'Please Please Me' / 'From Me to You'
08-02-64	'All My Loving' / 'This Boy'
15-02-64	'Roll Over Beethoven' / 'Please Mister Postman'
02-03-64	'Twist and Shout' / 'There's a Place'
16-03-64	'Can't Buy Me Love' / 'You Can't Do That'
23-03-64	'Do You Want to Know a Secret' /'Thank You Girl'
27-03-64	'Why' / 'Cry for a Shadow'
27-04-64	'Love Me Do' / 'P.S. I Love You'
21-05-64	'Sie Liebt Dich' / 'I'll Get You'
01-06-64	'Sweet Georgia Brown' / 'Take Out Some Insurance On Me'
06-07-64	'Ain't She Sweet' / 'Nobody's Child'
13-07-64	'A Hard Day's Night' / 'I Should Have Known Better'
20-07-64	'I'll Cry Instead' / 'Happy Just to Dance with You'
20-07-64	'And I Love Her' / 'If I Fell'
24-08-64	'Matchbox' / 'Slow Down'
15-02-65	'Eight Days a Week' / 'Don't Want to Spoil the Party'
19-07-65	'Help!' / 'I'm Down'
13-09-65	'Yesterday' / 'Act Naturally'
06-12-65	'We Can Work it Out' / 'Day Tripper'
21-02-66	'Nowhere Man' / 'What Goes On'
30-05-66	'Paperback Writer' / 'Rain'
08-08-66	'Yellow Submarine' / 'Eleanor Rigby'
13-02-67	'Penny Lane' / 'Strawberry Fields Forever'
17-07-67	'All You Need Is Love' / 'Baby You're a Rich Man'
27-11-67	'Hello Goodbye' / 'I Am the Walrus'
18-03-68	'Lady Madonna' / 'The Inner Light'
26-08-68	'Hey Jude' / 'Revolution'
05-05-68	'Get Back' / 'Don't Let Me Down'
04-06-69	'The Ballad of John and Yoko' / 'Old Brown Shoe'
06-10-69	'Come Together' / 'Something'
11-03-70	'Let It Be' / 'You Know My Name'
11-05-70	'The Long and Winding Road' / 'For You Blue'
31-05-76	'Got to Get You into My Life' / 'Helter Skelter'
08-06-76	'Ob-La-Di, Ob-La-Da' / 'Julia'
17-04-95	'Baby It's You' / 'I'll Follow the Sun'
	'Devil in Her Heart' / 'Boys'
12-12-95	'Free as a Bird' / 'Christmas Time'
04-03-96	'Real Love' / 'Baby's in Black'

PICTURE CREDITS

Right: Contact sheet with images of The Beatles' London Palladium show on October 13 1963.

Overleaf: The Beatles, as their fans will most commonly remember them, performing in October 1963.

WING 13 10 63